the Promise *of* Charity

Let Love
Guide
the Way

by Father Ralph W. Beiting

Father Beiting's previous CAP books include:

Promise of Hope... Fear Not, I Am With You Always

Promise of Faith... With Christ We Can Do All Things

God Can Move Mountains

Appalachia... A Special Place... A Bridge of Hope

Promises to Keep... A Vision for Appalachia

Dreams of Faith

Called to the Mountains... The Autobiography of Father Ralph W. Beiting

Frontier of the Heart... The Search for Heroes in Appalachia

Pilgrimage of a Country Preacher

A Journey to the Holy Land of Appalachia

A Family of My Own... The Dream I Thought I Missed

A Time of Crisis... A Time for Christ

Table of Contents

Dedication

A dedication is a way of saying thanks. It is a debt of gratitude that you want to pay to someone to whom you owe more than you could ever possibly repay.

Since this book explores the wonderful nature of love in my life, I want to dedicate the book to the women in my life. They have been examples of love from whom I gained a great deal.

The first woman I want to acknowledge is Jesus' mother Mary. She has shown me what love is all about. It is about Christ.

Never did she hesitate. He always came first. She held Him in her arms at Bethlehem and at Calvary as well. She took Him to the temple to be dedicated to His Father. She also fled with Him to Egypt.

She stood by Him always.

She has never left me, either. And so I wish to thank her as part of this dedication.

The next woman in my life was Martha, my mother. I was the oldest of her eleven children.

Children were her way of loving God. She would give Him many ambassadors, many helpers. It wasn't an easy gift to give in those great days of the Depression. But her total absorption in giving never failed. It shaped my life and my mind.

I remember so vividly other women — the nuns who taught me about the things of the earth and the things of God, and how they always had to be joined together. Loving and giving were the ingredients that would hold the two worlds together. I try to live the legacy of these women each day.

I'm now in my fiftieth year of service to the people of Appalachia. As I look back and try to remember the part love played in that story, I remember all the wonderful women who came —and still continue to come — as volunteers, and I sing their praises as well. Some stayed for a year, many for much longer periods of time. A few we have had for twenty-five years and more.

These women have been the embodiment of love. They have filled the mountains with grace without limit.

Finally, I want to acknowledge the wonderful donors who have supported the dream that I thought could not be reached. They have sacrificed and done without so that we could have enough.

Our donors haven't always seen our hills or explored our "hollows," but their love has touched people who had forgotten what love is all about.

Pope John Paul II expresses my feeling very well in his letter on the dignity of women:

> In God's eternal plan, woman is the one
> whom the ardor of love in the created
> world of persons first takes root.

Father Ralph W. Beiting

To the women who have helped me along the way, I dedicate this book.

The Christian Appalachian Project 2000

Fifty years ago, Father Ralph W. Beiting was called to Appalachia to build church communities and ease the pain caused by poverty. In 1964, he founded an interdenominational Christian organization called the Christian Appalachian Project (CAP) Inc. By offering long-term, self-help solutions to the problems that hold Appalachia's people back, CAP gives the poor a chance to work themselves out of poverty and to see themselves as they truly are: the people of God.

CAP provides educational programs for children and adults, home repair assistance, business development programs, elderly visitation programs, emergency relief assistance, and so many other efforts. With over seventy programs and activities, CAP brings hope and peace to those in need.

Through the generous work of thousands of volunteers, hundreds of local workers, and a host of loyal supporters from all over the country, CAP has become one of the largest relief organizations in America, and a pioneer in the development of programs to defeat poverty and inspire hope.

Prologue

I began this book the Monday before Thanksgiving. This will be the last of the three books written in preparation for the millennium. The first two were on "Faith" and "Hope" — two of the three things that last, in the words of Saint Paul.

This volume is my attempt to show how the third of these — Love — has entered my life and kept me in the service of the people of Appalachia for fifty years.

When I was in college, I had the part of Richard II in Shakespeare's play. At the end of the play, Richard, held prisoner in a dungeon, is about to be murdered. "Love," he muses, "is like a strange sounding word in this all-hating world." He speaks from despair.

I would like to speak in this book with faith and hope as my foundation. I realize love has been cheapened by our modern world and its literature and media. Love has stood for selfishness, for mere physical and emotional gratification that centers on "me" — on what I want — and not on the one whom I love and whom I should serve.

The contrast between today's shallow understanding of love and love's true meaning struck me again not long ago.

In October, I was in Washington, DC to receive an honor from Catholic University, my alma mater. I was to be acknowledged as the Alumnus of the Year.

During that week, I visited, among other things, the Lincoln Memorial. Lincoln is someone dear to me because he was born in Kentucky and stayed here until he was ten years old. He was a pioneer not only here, but in Illinois and in the nation as a whole.

But most of all, I think I care for Lincoln because of his love. As we all know, he was asked to lead a country when hatred over the issue of slavery was the most divisive element in the nation. And his whole dream was to heal. He would bind together the nation, and at the same time he would try to set those free who had been deprived of justice and liberty.

He was a man who, even on the battlefield of Gettysburg, would cry out that these dead must not have died in vain. That we, as the living, must continue their work, and that we must bring forth love so that their death and suffering may not have been in vain.

And even in the second inaugural address that he made a few months before his life was taken, he said that, with malice towards none and charity and love towards all, let us bind together this nation once again. He was a man who wanted to do something to heal, to bring about peace and joy. They would take his life before he could bring it about. Although tragic, I think Lincoln's death had some positive outcome in that it allowed people to see that love was more than a word, more than a political phrase. It was something enduring and heartfelt.

On that day in October, I preached for well over an hour in front of the Lincoln Memorial, as the tourists came and went.

In November, I visited and preached at Memphis, Tennessee. I went to the Lorraine Motel where the Reverend Martin Luther King, Jr. was shot and killed. It is now the Civil Rights Museum for Reverend Martin Luther King, Jr.

Rev. King witnessed great injustice in our nation. He saw people deprived of all kinds of good that they should have had by right. He could have been angry, calling out for violence and striking back. He and his people had been deeply wronged.

But it was love that was going to motivate him and to bring about the things that he saw were needed.

He said he had a dream. And that dream was that all men should be treated with love, irrespective of their color or their national origins. That the image of God in each of us needed to be loved. And I think that is the heritage he gave to us all, letting us know that love was far more important than violence and getting even.

About that same time, I preached at Alice Lloyd College in a little place called Pippa Passes, KY. Back in the 1910s, a lady out of Massachusetts had come there to die. She was told she had four months to live and yet she refused to feel sorry for herself.

She came to this isolated area with the dream and hope that she could bring education to the children, so that they might grow strong and tall. And while she was there, her husband deserted her for another woman. She was left with her mother and was later joined by another wonderful lady, June Buchanan.

The name of this inspired woman was Alice Lloyd. Despite what she'd been told, she lived in that place for the rest of her life — another thirty or more years — and there she founded a school that grew to a four-year college.

She taught us that love is really what is important. And I think the students at Alice Lloyd College have taken the message to heart because such a great percentage of them go back to the mountains to serve their people.

This morning I read the story of Edith Stein. She was a young Jewish woman who, finding solace in the Catholic Faith, joined the church and eventually became a Carmelite Nun.

At that time, Hitler was ruling Germany so she was driven out to Holland. When the German armies came into Holland, she was taken and put on a train that would take her to Auschwitz and execution.

Never in all this time was she an angry woman. She wrote to others and encouraged them, saying that they needed to suffer as Jesus had suffered. Only with love could they redeem the world. It was going to take love to overcome the terrible hatred of Nazism and Hitler.

At a time of immense hatred, this tremendous lady showed the world that only love could overcome.

All of these people gave their lives so that love may endure. They all followed another great man who did the same.

It was Christ who said that only when he was lifted up on the cross would he draw all men to himself. A greater love than this no man would have, that he would lay down his life for his friends.

All of these people have left a great example of love. But what good is an example if we do not use or follow it? As I said, it is for us, the living, to dedicate ourselves to the task that still remains. It is up to us to see that these dead may not have died in vain, that their example of love may not fade away.

In fifty years I have seen so much selfishness, greed and anger, women and children victimized and money and power pervading all things. I've seen people running to protect themselves, to take care of themselves, to make themselves number one. People who reached out in anger to get even and to punish those who stood in their way. I think back to the words that Saint Paul said to the Corinthians, words so powerful, so very much needed:

"If I have all the eloquence of men or of angels but speak without love, I am simply a gong booming or a cymbal clashing. If I have the gift of prophecy, understanding all the mysteries and knowing everything, and if I have faith to move mountains, but I have not love, then I am nothing at all.

"If I give away all that I possess, piece by piece let them take my body to burn it, but without love, it will do me no good whatsoever.

"Love is always patient and kind. It is never jealous. Love is never boastful or conceited. It is never rude or selfish. It does not take offense and is not resentful. Love takes no pleasure in other people's sins; it delights in the truth. It is always ready to excuse, to trust, to hope, and to endure whatever comes. Love does not come to an end, but if there are gifts of prophecy, the time will come when they must fail. The gift of language will not continue forever. And for knowledge, the time will come when it must fail. For our knowledge isn't perfect and our prophesizing isn't perfect, but once perfection comes, all imperfect things will disappear.

"When I was a child I used to talk like a child and think like a child and argue like a child, but now I am a man, all childish ways are put aside. Now we see a dim reflection in a mirror, but soon we shall be seeing face to face. The knowledge that I have now isn't perfect, but I know it shall be when I am fully known. In short, there are three things that last: faith, hope, and love. And the greatest of these is love."

So now I ask you: Will you come and walk with me through these pages? Hopefully, we shall truly feel God's love.

Chapter 1 The Love of Family

A special clock given to me almost a year ago tells me that there are 30 days, 15 minutes and 30 seconds left before one millennium ends and another begins. I like it when Americans reflect on the century about to end. After all, I have 76 years invested in it.

This has been called the most violent century in the history of the human race. Never before has mankind sought to destroy itself as it has in this century.

It has left a terrible cloud hanging over the coming millennium. People live in fear.

We fear for our houses, for our money, for our pensions, for our cars, and all the rest. We worry about our health, our marriages, and our children. We fear for our very lives and safety. We even fear old age, a time of wonder that has become, instead, a time of fear.

I was once invited to speak at a local college. As I talked about God and how he had to be a part of our lives, I asked my young listeners, "What do you think, as college students, is the greatest cause of fear?"

And a young man immediately raised his hand and said, "It is family."

He said, "I don't know what family is all about anymore. My mother and father divorced when I was a little child. They have remarried and have new families, and I don't know where my loyalty lies. I am barely part of their lives anymore. It leaves me wondering, how can I ever find love?"

Then one of the teachers who was teaching and listening to the discussion said, "I'm also afraid. My husband works and I teach here, and the television has become our child's guardian. I wonder how we can ever help him and others grow up in love when they see so little of us and so much of what is on television?"

I left that college campus full of worry myself. Family, the center of peace and love, was being decimated by modern culture.

However, about a month later, while I was visiting some of the CAP programs that help the people of Appalachia help themselves, I spent six days traveling around listening to amazing stories.

I was in Pulaski County, KY. We had purchased land there many years before. Now one of CAP's buildings has been set aside as a temporary shelter for children and women who have been abused.

I saw children not quite sure if they should come out of their room or not, as they wondered whether they'd be safe. And I saw women who hardly ever smiled.

And yet as I talked to the staff, I sensed love and excitement there.

The staff was exploring the idea of having houses for these women and children to live in after their stay at the shelter. It was the staff's attempt to reach into the unknown and bring about a better tomorrow.

I also visited a child development center on that same trip. I spoke to some of the parents and some of the older people who were out on the porch. They were telling stories of how they had gone through so much misery in their lives — and not only misery from poverty — but misery from lack of love and families. They were at the child development center to see if in some small way they could reinforce the work of its teachers. They wanted to let the children know that this was a good place — and that hopefully joy would be coming into their lives.

At the college, at the spouse abuse shelter, and at the child development center, I kept hearing the same message: In the family, where there should be security, love, and dedication, there was anxiety and fear.

If there is a single word that can counteract the fear in the family, it is love. For doesn't God's word say that love can cast out fear? Our Lord has given us the real answer. We have to begin to learn how to love before fear can be eliminated.

Tonight I sit overlooking Yatesville Lake. It is the site of a camp I started especially for families. Kids are wonderful and parents are a blessing, but they need to be brought together in love to a special place that can guide them to grow and increase in love. I sit here praying for the wisdom that will enable me to write the chapters on family love in a way that will enable each of you who read these pages to grow in the love that family was meant to instill.

I cannot help but remember my own family. I remember the time that my brother, Don, and I were fishing in the Ohio River. We had our lines out and a gentleman came along with a boat and tore them up. And when we protested, he came back threatening to punish us for calling out and yelling at him. But as he pulled the boat on shore and came charging towards us, my father came down the bank.

I was never so glad to see my father in all my life!

He told the man that he had better mend his ways and go on down the river because there'd be trouble if he tried to harm us.

Even though we were unjustly accused by this gentleman, he would have undoubtedly given us a good beating. But there was my father, standing and protecting his family.

I remember my mother's last day alive. She was in the living room of our house. We were about to take her to the nursing home when she looked up at me, the oldest of her children, and said, "Will you hug me? Will you give me a hug? Will you hold me close?"

I never will forget that day and the tears that came down my face and moistened her face. What more could she have asked? What more could she have given me as her time came to an end than to ask for a hug?

I remember the mass for my 50th anniversary of ordination. It was a wonderful mass. My nieces and great-nieces and nephews were all there to help honor God in thanksgiving for my 50 years of priesthood. Then came the procession of bringing up the wine and host. My oldest sister, Dorothy, and my brother, Paul, had been assigned to that, but both of them had just come back from the hospital and they were so weak and so feeble that no one thought they were up to this task.

But they came up, hand in hand, one holding on to the other for support as they made the difficult journey. To see those two, so feeble and yet so dedicated a part of my family, was something I shall never forget. Their love prompted them to do these things.

Our family is much like every other family; we don't always see eye-to-eye. With 11 strong individuals and their families, each one has a slightly different emphasis on this value or that, different ways of doing things, but this past year love has united us as never before.

My brother, Jimmy, was a bricklayer by profession. He married a wonderful young woman named Joan, and God blessed them with seven children. Jimmy and Joan are now in their middle and late sixties. A few years back, Joan was diagnosed with cancer. Due to her illness, she had surgery three times this past year.

Along with the cancer came the beginnings of Alzheimer's Disease. Joan feels so terrible that she can't remember all the things she wishes she could recall. But I don't think there was ever a time that she was loved as much as she is now.

Jimmy has become a model to us all. He cares for Joan in so many beautiful little ways, taking the hurts and offering them back with love, and taking the love and repaying it time and time again. We see their suffering, and yet we see how love has overcome the suffering and made it a beautiful thing.

I think of my sister-in-law, Rose, who was married to my brother Ray. He died from Lou Gehrig's disease. For two years, Rose cared for him as his strength gradually left day by day.

Ray was such a strong person himself. When you asked ask him how he was, he never told you how he felt. He always told you he was fine. He was happy that he had found love and, despite the shortcomings of the physical side, there was no lack of meaning in his life.

I think, too, of my sister Mary Lou and her husband Jim. They had three children. They lost their last child and their second child, Kevin, was afflicted by all sorts of difficulties and was handicapped all the days of his life. Yet, in spite of it, he was such a cheerful young boy, always doing kind and caring things. Then came that tragic night when he was just 21 and he fell asleep face-down and suffocated.

It was such a terrible shock to us all. Yet throughout their grief, if you dropped Mary Lou and Jim a card or gave them a call, they never hesitated to express how grateful they were that Kevin had been a part of their lives. For in his short, kind life, he had helped them to grow in love for one another, as well as for him.

My Aunt Mary is now in her eighties. She was married to Bill, the youngest of my uncles. Only seven years separated me from Aunt Mary.

For the last 25 years of their marriage, Uncle Bill could hardly do anything for himself because of a stroke. Aunt Mary worked with him and served him and cared for him all those years, and never saw it as a burden. Never was there a time when it was something heroic. It was just love.

The sparkle in her eye let you know that there was no problem here; it was merely her way of thanking God that she still had him. And now that he has gone, she gives herself entirely to the service of others. She takes the elderly in her community shopping and to church, and she does all kinds of marvelous things for them.

She is never lonely because she is full of love. She goes forth and brings God to all she meets.

I remember others who are part of my family as well – although not necessarily related to me by blood. They are the members of my family that have come through the church.

For more than 30 years, I served the church in the central and south eastern sections of Kentucky. There I made friends that I have loved for many, many years.

I got a call the other day from a good friend of mine. His mother, Barbara Feldman, had just died. He wanted to know if I could come there, have mass, and offer prayers. I assured him that I certainly would. So, I went that day into the church I had built so many years before and I was surrounded by other members of the Feldman family and many of the other original parishioners as well.

As I went through the talk and remembered many things that had happened, tears filled the eyes of the congregation. And later on, as we had refreshments after the mass and the ceremonies at the cemetery, we thanked each other for what we had been to one another. We had, even at a funeral, an opportunity to renew love, dedication, and commitment to one another.

I remember, too, the many families that I've helped over the years. For example, Farrin and Marie had a rash of misfortunes including their home catching on fire, their well drying up and their children falling ill. To help them out, CAP gave them help to repair their home and the means to get a job. And then I put them in charge of renovating a school that CAP is trying to bring back to life and offer as a service to many others.

In fact, we just got a whole host of letters from students at Notre Dame University. They had been helping fix up the old school, and they wrote to say what it meant to them to be associated with Farrin and Marie, who had shown them so much care and love, and how they enjoyed this couple's children.

I think maybe that's what education is about: for these college students to go away from their schools and come and see the real world where family, love, and dedication are still vital and strong.

And as I visit the various volunteers that have been coming for more than 50 years, I see so many of them who came as strangers and found love among themselves and have joined their love in marriage. Now many of them, like Kathy from Massachusetts and Tony from Ohio, live in Kentucky working in various industries or other volunteer programs. And the love of these former CAP volunteers has produced many children.

As I look upon these new families, I can't help but think, "Thank you, Lord, in letting me be single and not letting me have the children myself, but rather for letting me be instrumental in bringing so many together who love and care for each other!"

I think of two others who met as volunteers: Fritz, who is in his seventies, and Arleen, who is in her late sixties. I celebrated their wedding up in Maryland not long ago.

Love has made their life sparkle and given them a vitality that they had not had for many years. What brought them happiness and peace? It was not the youthful ways, it wasn't the jobs they had, it was not even the religion they shared. It was love.

As I think about all these things and try to put them down on paper, I pause for a moment to step outside my little trailer, this little hideaway overlooking the lake. The full moon shines so brightly overhead. As I look up at the moon, more memories come back, but they are not always pleasant.

I remember a little girl who lives on the street where my secretary lives. The girl is 14 years old and hasn't seen her father but once or twice in her entire life. Her mother is in jail. She is being raised by a grandmother who finds it difficult to keep her in check.

Now we have learned she is four months pregnant. What shall happen to that child and to the child's child? One can't help but worry, think and pray about that.

I remember a lady I met this summer while going down the Ohio River, "street preaching" to people on the river fronts from the deck of a boat. We were in Madison, IN and I had just finished preaching for the night and gone on shore to thank the people who had listened. I noticed a plainly dressed lady standing there. She was watching every move I made. I finally went over to her and said, "Ma'am, may I be of help to you?"

She said, "May I tell you my story? It was at this spot nearly a year ago that my husband dropped me out of the car, beat me up, broke my arm, bloodied my face and let me lie here by the side of the river. People came by and I was taken to the hospital where my arm was set, but he threatened me to never come near him again.

"I come down to this river place nearly every day to pray, and sometimes I talk to people about trying to love God because I found so much love among people. And I had prayed to the Lord, 'Why, Lord, do you let all these gambling boats come by? Why do you allow all these pleasure crafts that people just simply enjoy and sometimes misuse for pleasure? Why can't you send a boat down that says something about your Son?'"

And then she said to me, "I was here just a week ago tonight praying for that, and here this evening you came and you were preaching about Christ and his love and how we have to find out who we are and that is the people of God. I just want to thank you — you have refurnished me with love. And I want to thank you in another way as well."

Then she reached into the pockets of this crumpled old dress and handed me a handful of paper money.

I said, "No, Ma'am, I don't need that."

She said, "But I do. Will you please take it?"

So, I took it. When I got on the boat later that evening, I saw that it was two one-dollar bills all crumpled up. I'm sure that it was the last two dollars she had. She was trying to regain love, and the way in which she was going to do it was by helping others and doing something that was very special.

I think of all the problems that foster parents face when they agree to take on foster children. Oftentimes, terrible things have happened to these foster children. Many of the girls have been sexually abused by their own families — by fathers mostly. Looking at the difficulties these children have, one can only wonder how their foster families can in only a few months undo the harm that has gone on before.

Then there is the lady who shot her husband just a couple of weeks ago. She had run away from home and then, in a moment of despair, went back and shot her husband. The police finally caught her. Hopefully, the man won't die. As I pray for them both, I wonder: why should two people who were once so much in love want to do violence to each other, to hurt or even kill?

I think about all these people and sometimes I just cry out, "Why, Lord? Why must love be such a stranger in our world? Can't you inspire people? Can't you get things moving?"

I look back and think of all the hope that has gone by in this past century and I say, "Lord, this has been such a bad time. Love has truly become a strange-sounding word in this all-hating world. Can't you do better as this new millennium is about to start? Can't you make a new beginning? Can't you be creative again, Lord?"

As I calm down for a moment, our Lord's voice comes slowly, yet firmly, to my ears. "You always want to blame someone, don't you — to find fault? Haven't you realized this yet: it is better to light a candle than to curse the darkness? Can't you see what my people need is an example of love?

"Look at my example. It is awesome. You need to show a better example of love. It is your task. Don't blame me.

"Do you call your brothers and sisters on their birthdays and wedding anniversaries to tell them that you love them? Do you talk to your people about love? Do you take the time to prepare the young for marriage? Do they know what love really means, or are you only concerned about the paperwork, and all the legal documents and ceremonies?

"Do you get families together who are truly in love and ask them to bring in other families where love is only lukewarm? You could be doing so much if you got loving families to work with other families to bring about the same kind of love in their lives. You have got to start with yourself.

"While I'm at it," the Lord said, "I would like for you to be more positive. You are not as bad as you think, and the world is not quite as awful as you sometimes imagine.

"Take a moment to look again at the full moon. Do you see reflected in it the foster home you have supported over the years? Through these foster families, you have saved many a child and enriched so many lives in so many ways.

"And look, if you will, at the homes you have repaired over these last 50 years. Look at all the comfort you have brought in where there was misery and despair. Look at all the warmth and the sense of belonging that has come about because people have places so much better to live in.

"Look at all the food and clothing you have distributed in 50 years! You have seen a mountain of food and a mountain of clothing go out to people who thought no one cared or loved them.

"And look at the camps, youth centers, and Bible schools that you have started. Do you remember?

"How many times, around a campfire, did children learn from you to dream the impossible dream? Learn that people would come and help them if they only would persevere.

"How about the youth centers that took in children failing in school? With the help of the volunteers, the children changed their lives and began to dream. And the Bible schools, where the children learned to pray and learned the stories from my sacred scripture? They learned to know me a little more and care for me a little better. Remember all these things as you look upon this full moon.

"I hope that you remember the visit that you had at Mount Vernon at the Child Development Center not so long ago. Did you see all the fathers that came that evening to be present with their children? They came after work, oftentimes in work clothes, but they wanted to be there to let their children know that they were loved, that this was important, and that they wanted them to continue their studies.

"Look at the houses that you are setting up for abused spouses and their families. They are unable to return to their original homes, but you are helping them to get individual homes for themselves where they will have direction and the support of others.

"These things are part of the answer, and they are the way in which love will come back into your lives.

"Look at the volunteers who come and discover a different view of love. These people came because of romantic ideas that they were going to save the poor and be a part of a new world. Yet, you have made them understand that it is not romance that will make the world different, it is going to be love. They're going to have to work hard and to sacrifice, and they'll have to call others in to be of assistance.

"You have had nearly 50,000 volunteers over the last 50 years and you have made love a little more meaningful to all of them.

"Look, too, at the work that you do with the ministers and their counseling for the youth. You have been deep in your faith and love for the church and you have never turned your back on ministers from other faiths.

"You have reached out with love to all of them, and together you have worked and made it possible for them to reach those children and elderly whom you could never touch. Because of your help and enthusiasm, you have reached beyond where you could ever have gone, thanks to the goodness of these other ministers.

"I must tell you that you are far from where I want you to be. You're not the kind of person yet that you ought to be.

"But you and CAP have made a great difference in my mountains these past 50 years. You have been a

rainbow of hope. You have been the evening star that
begins to illuminate the evening. I have come to count
on you, weak and frail as you are.

"What I'm asking you now is to keep the torch of
love alive. It will draw many towards a better view of
life. Your major task is to be an example of love. If you
are that, then other people will see and follow."

By this time it is getting cold out here on the lake. I
lay down my pen and go inside my little trailer, where I
will spend the evening.

As I get inside where it's a little warmer, I sit in a
chair and just simply say, "Lord, please don't forget me.
Keep talking to me. I so need your love and I will keep
on trying. Lord, without you I am nothing, but with you
I am all things. Please, please let me know love, and
love me..."

I am tired. As I prepare to go to bed, I pick out the
book I have on Christian heroes. And tonight I read
again about Edith Stein. She knew her death at
Auschwitz was only a train-ride away. She offered her
life to God in love for the well-being of her Jewish family and friends and for all others whose lives would be
unjustly taken.

That was love. The greatest there is. And she only
asked God for the privilege of giving her life in love to
Him so that others might have a chance. To offer your
sufferings up, when you care more for others than you
do for yourself — that is what love is all about.

As I turn out the light I pray, dear reader, that you
will pray for me, that the love you have may come to me.

I turn over in bed and add, "Please Lord, help me to remember that I am a member of every family in the world. Let love come from me to reach them all. Help me bring love to my mountains for the people that I love."

I am over in bed and add, "Please, God help me remember that I am a member of your family in this world. Let love come from my heart to them all. Help my giving love to my neighbor, that the people that I love...

Chapter 2   The Love of Work

As this century comes to a close and we look back on all the problems that impacted our human family, hardly any have had the importance that work has had.

On the world scene, we had communism and its call to all workers to unite and cast off the yoke of their oppressors.

The proletariat had to revolt in the 20th century. They had to be free. But communism rejected God as unnecessary, even injurious, to the cause of the working poor. Work would be rewarded only when they formed the powerful state that would guide them and control all elements of society.

We have seen more than 70 years of this communism at work in our world. In recent days we have seen the collapse of its theory. The society that was to make the laborers free enslaved them. It took away their freedom, and their final lot was worse than the first.

Millions were killed in this struggle to know and understand the value and dignity of work.

Communism would never have come about, however, if the workers had not been abused.

A materialistic society valued work as a means of acquiring great wealth. The cheaper the labor, the greater the profit. A worker was not a person. He was merely a spoke in the wheel that turned out profit.

Consumerism, even today, guides so much the way we treat the working poor. Adults, even children, in Africa, Asia, and South America are exploited so that the rich can get richer.

I was in Philadelphia at the Presidential Summit called by the President and overseen by Colin Powell. Our goal was to get two million volunteers by the year 2000 to monitor children and to give children safe places to live.

In one of the discussions, a young man from Taiwan held up his hand. He said, "When did we ever address the nature of work?" He talked about sports shoes, particularly the various brands that basketball athletes wear. He said, "In my country, my people are exploited. We are asked to work for a few dollars a day and the shoes are sold at a great profit here in America. And the profit comes so that the athletes and their sponsors grow richer. Yet the poor people who produced the shoes are not given enough on which to live."

A silence fell over the hall. And I think everyone understood what our capitalism, our consumerism, our great television advertising and sports fanaticism have done to the poor of the world.

Even in this country, which I think has the best of records on the treatment of workers, we still see the shadow of Third World labor. The work of immigrants is the only cheap labor we have today. The number of immigrants from the Hispanic world and from other impoverished places is growing, as they try to find enough to live on and support their families. In fact, even as I write these pages, Chinese workers are literally dying to be smuggled into this country. Many are dead from maltreatment by the time they arrive.

I remember so well the days of the Great Depression in our own nation. When there was no work, the solution seemed to be welfare. All the poor had to do was to get in line and hold out their hands. All they had to do was give up their initiative, and they would be cared for. We turned the once proud and independent people into recipient wards of the bureaucracy.

None of these systems — not communism, not unrestrained capitalism, not the patriarchal state — has truly understood the nature of work and the worker.

Work cannot be understood unless God has a place in the world. Only when God is involved can we understand the value of the worker. Who is this creature, man? He is not function, not a force to be used. He has the stamp of God on him. He can, in truth, call God his father and Christ his brother. What we do to Him, we do to Christ, even if the worker is the least of God's children.

In God's plans for the well-being of the whole human family, work is a necessary part. Our first work was to watch over and guide all of creation. This mon-

umental task was given not as punishment, but rather
to have us represent God Himself. There was something divine about work. It was carrying out the way of
God and the plan of God.

Even after the fall of man in the garden when selfishness ruled the moment, God said that man could
participate in his own redemption by working. The
effort and the sacrifice could be a great value if it was
done in love for the good of all and the glory of God.
Man would earn his bread by the sweat of his brow,
but it would be the way in which he would help to
bring himself back to God.

God wanted His children back home. He wanted
them to be with Him again. He wanted the bridge
repaired and the road made straight that led to Him.
While He would do the major work through His son,
we could participate in bridge-building and road making
by means of work that was the expression of love.

As I look back on my pilgrimage of 50 years, I am
proud to see that this idea of man — his work, his dignity — cannot be brought into reality without Christ
and his love.

Fifty years ago, I didn't want to start another political force nor another human services organization. I
wanted a group of people of deep faith who would seek
to bring about the plan of God for all mankind.

Work was an indispensable part of this plan, and it
had to be work permeated with love.

I looked at the problems I faced. In Jackson
County, the poorest of my original four counties, there

were no jobs except those in the service industry and farming. These alone could not solve the problem. We needed to create work that could be marketed outside of our area and bring in additional funds.

I selected the following areas for new jobs: dairy, sawmills, greenhouses, Christmas wreaths, and woodworking. Their creation would demand hard work from me and from those who joined me.

As I think about it now after many years, I know that at that time no businessman would have tried to do these things. My programs were idealistic. We didn't have the resources necessary to carry them through.

Yet look what has come about. George Purcell, the first worker to join me in the Christian Appalachian Project, took on the responsibility of a dairy farm. We had to clear land and build fences. And we had to do a great number of other things. We didn't know that there was any other answer but to work and bring about all that we could.

Today the dairy farm has grown beyond our wildest dreams. George Purcell has created many exciting new ventures in marketing dairy products. He has also become a member of the National Dairy Association — and this past Christmas convinced the association to donate a great amount of cheese that we shared with people through our Christmas baskets.

The dairy farm led in turn to another project. I approached a young man from the Bardstown area, Melvin Marks, and his wife. I said to them, "Will you undertake a sawmill operation?" It wasn't really a sawmill at first. It was just simply putting a chainsaw to desirable timber so that we might expand the farm's pastures. The wood was sold as firewood for a little recompense.

And yet today, Melvin still operates the sawmill, turning out patterns for building barns and other structures. When timber is cleared, new trees are planted. The land rewards our work and is a blessing because of that.

When I talked to Dale Anastasia, a young man from Rochester, NY, I asked him, "Based on your studies at the University of Kentucky, what sorts of things could we do here?"

His response was, "Well, I think that a good business idea could be greenhouses. You see, Kentucky has so little land to till, and greenhouses could enhance production dramatically."

So, we began by erecting a simple little greenhouse with plastic coverings. Today it extends to over an acre under glass, and its products are sold in four different states. Dale is now using the Internet to help sell the products. This is an unbelievable kind of development that is here not because of economic ingenuity, but because we felt we ought to do something creative and that could be brought about with God's help.

Other people like Ben Tincher also came to my assistance in those early years. I said to Ben, "We need to make Christmas wreaths. We need to take the boughs of pine trees that are being cut down anyway and turn them into things of beauty."

He responded, "I have an old tobacco barn that is waiting to be used." And so it was that we wrapped the barn in plastic, put gravel on the floor, brought in a heater from a trailer, and had a place where women and men could work producing Christmas wreaths.

This business is now a separate corporation that has created economic development for more than 25 years.

It was to Charlie Simpsen, Marvin Schuler and Tony Lacada that we said, "Will you come and start a wood-working shop? Will you take the raw materials and turn them into things of beauty whether they are dulcimers, chopping blocks, book-ends, or various other things?"

Now, the shop is still in operation and still producing products that are sold.

Each one of these ventures succeeded, and each one of them today is a private business on its own. How did this all come about? It took work. And, some of that work took a lot of asking!

I had to go and ask for many things. I had to ask for some of the tools from a company in Cincinnati. I had to ask for so many other things necessary for the livestock, the sawmill and other areas. We had to get started. We simply said to the prospective donors, "We have a dream and we think that work is one of the answers for getting us to that dream. And if we pursue this dream with the love of God, then God will be on our side and we shall succeed."

We planned as far as we were able. We sat down and talked with one another and we determined the best way to present these ideas and pursue them.

But what we also did was to say to one another, "We must have enthusiasm. We are not going to succeed if we think that failure is around the corner."

What we said to ourselves is that the enthusiasm has to come from the fact that we have to rely on Christ. Christ made a promise. He said that, "With Me and with love you can do all things. Only when you have no love, when you have no enthusiasm, when you have no Me, will you fail."

If you continue to bring love into your life, you will make a world of difference.

Gene Hensley came to me when we were in the process of building the Christmas Wreath Program. After working in California, he'd decided to move back to his home county in Kentucky and do something to help his people. I gave him a job directing the Christmas wreath operation.

He got so involved in so many other activities that he helped to bring about the Jackson County Empowerment Zone, which enables federal money to come in and create jobs.

When we talk about those early days, our feeling was that with God watching we could do great things.

Grant Satterly with the Mountain Economic Development Fund has since taken over the Christmas wreath operation and is making more wreaths this year than last. He has continued to expand the operation and, in doing so, has helped other businesses.

Just a few months ago, I had the opportunity to meet a fellow named Jerry Weaver. He is originally from Clay County, KY and he went to school in Jackson County at the Annville Institute operated by the Dutch Reform Church.

Jerry gave himself to that school. He was trained and taught there and finished high school, and yet he knew that he was not going to be able to pursue college. Instead, he went to Dayton, OH and learned tool-making. And then he began to work in places like Alabama and various other states, and success followed him.

What he had in mind, though, was to come back to Jackson County and do something for the community that had given him such enthusiasm for learning. Today he has established several jobs in Jackson County, as well as several corporations that are serving worldwide companies.

Furthermore, he has given jobs to people who never thought they would have one.

And why was all of this created and shared? It was because of love — what he had received as a young man — and how he wanted to return that love in a very special way.

I think this is one of the great and wondrous stories of our time. It shows what love can overcome.

In quiet moments (when I find time to enjoy them!), I sit back in my chair and think of the one who brought all of this about. It was not myself nor any of the aforementioned men. It was Jesus.

He hangs on a cross in this little enclosed porch of mine that also serves as an office. During these moments I say to him, "Lord, there are so many times when I didn't think it would work – that there was no way it would succeed. How can I ever thank you for all the help you have given me, the wisdom you have furnished, the love you have poured out upon me and those that assist me?"

I think, here I was, just an ordinary young man coming out of the Depression himself, coming into this land of Appalachia that is tormented with so much poverty.

It was a blessing to come up with all those ideas that not even a powerful businessman would have dared to touch.

I say simply, "Lord, how can I ever thank you? You have not only brought about new opportunities to work, but you have also made the spiritual nature of our work known to all."

This is so true. The young that we have trained are seeing that this work — true work done in love and respect for one another — is a way in which they can cooperate with God to bring about a more just and loving world.

I say to him as I look at him hanging on that cross, "How can I ever thank you, Lord? How can I ever thank you?"

And I hear him speak: "Just listen to me and follow my plans for you. You don't always have to know all the answers. Just know that I will reveal them in due time. You simply need to keep the dream alive.

"You need to talk to all about jobs and work and love. I will raise up people to help you. I will give you — and others — the means of bringing this about. I want you to remember that I love these people more than you ever will. I have a plan. All I need are people who will love Me enough to do whatever I ask."

I am so taken by God who speaks to me so! He has wisdom. He knows all things and can bring about everything that is good. And what He is saying to me is, I don't expect you to have all the answers. I have them. All you need to do is to be ready to do My will and to follow, even though the course looks impossible – even though there seems to be no logical answer to it all. Remember, I brought things out of nothing, and I have preserved the world and made it a wondrous place. Pay attention. Listen.

And I simply say to him, "Lord. Speak. Your servant heareth."

It is late again and I think to myself, you have worked hard all your life. You don't have anything in the bank to show that your work has been a success. But you have surely made a difference. You have created an atmosphere of hope. You have been insisting upon faith, and if you continue to be an example of love, day in and day out, it shall all come about, for God is there.

The Bible isn't yours, it's His. The people aren't yours, they are His. And He loves them more than you can ever imagine. He will move and motivate — and there shall come a better tomorrow.

"Lord," I say, "please, please give me courage. Please give me that enthusiasm. Please grant that I may never tire in doing good."

I turn off the lights and head for the bedroom and once again I take out my book of heroes. I think of Christopher Columbus. And I think of all the problems he faced, such as his crew wanting to commit mutiny and go back to the world they knew and sail no longer into the unknown. He never gave up hope. He came at last to this new world and there he offered the body and blood of Christ, and prayers that this would be a new paradise, a new era. By all reckonings he should not have succeeded, by all wisdom he should have turned back. But because he didn't, there is a place called America where hope is a wondrous gift.

And I say to Christopher, "I hope that I have the perseverance you had. I hope that I may have the tenacity to never say the story has ended."

And he answers, "Pray. Put your faith in God and not in yourself. Do not grow strong because of others, but because of and with Him. Truly you can do all things."

"Lord," I say, "thank you for your gift of work. Thank you for the sanctifying grace that it produces within me. Thank you for the love that motivates it. May we work side-by-side to bring about even more love for tomorrow."

&

Chapter 3 The Love of Sharing

As I write this chapter, it is January. The temperature
last night got to 2 above zero, which is very low for us
here in Eastern Kentucky.

A fireplace keeps me warm. I look out the window.
The Louisa Fork of the Big Sandy River is covered by
a sheet of ice. The afternoon sun is making its retreat
behind a cloud that threatens to bring us even more
snow.

I marvel at the sight. It stirs up memories of long
ago, taking me back to the days of the Great
Depression.

At one point, two of my brothers were in the
hospital in Cincinnati. My family had so little, not even
a dime to pay the toll to cross the bridge to visit them.

Yet when we stopped at the homes of our aunts
and uncles on the way, they would share some food
and give clothing to the children. Oftentimes an uncle
would silently slip a bill into my father's hand.

I was old enough to know that my family was truly
a sharing one.

I remember Grandfather Hiance, my mother's
father, walking over a mile to our place just to trim

back the grape vines in our backyard. Gardening was one of his strongest skills. He shared his talents so that the grapes would have an even better yield the following season.

During his visits, he always delighted us kids by slipping a Necco wafer into our hands. As he did, he always had a big smile on his face. We knew it was because he was glad to be sharing.

My Grandfather Beiting visited almost every day. He also helped us with the gardening, and even went so far as to buy us a Sears & Roebuck tractor to plow and cultivate the land.

I remember a woman who lived across the fields from our house. She was always offering me an odd job: cleaning out her chicken house, shoveling, raking or plowing. I knew that she didn't really need to have those chores done – she could have done all those things herself. But she wanted to share and reach out to a family which had so many children and so many needs.

Then there were the neighbors up and down the road where we lived. Whenever there were some extra vegetables from their gardens – potatoes, tomatoes, corn, peas, beans – they offered them to us.

Besides the neighbors and the relatives, there was also the local parish priest. He always took the younger fellows to ball games. Afterward, on the way home, he would always have us stop for ice cream.

My high school was about seven miles from my home. We couldn't afford the bus fare, but people would always kindly stop by and offer me a ride to school.

At the school, priests went out of their way to offer after-school odd jobs, helping me pay for my tuition and books.

My parents provided a model of complete sharing and giving that is impossible to describe. We didn't have a lot of every kind of new gadget. Instead, we had that old-fashioned thing called love.

Among us brothers and sisters, the rule of helping one another out wasn't written down.

Rather, it was simply a part of our life. If somebody needed help, that's what each one of us reached out to do.

In August of 1941, I entered the seminary. During that wondrous time, it was our privilege each day to read sections of the sacred scriptures. What I discovered was not just the philosophical or the theological precepts. What impressed me most were the stories of heroes.

I think of a man like Abraham. He had wealth and prestige in the city of Ur on the Persian Gulf. He had all the things that a man could have wanted.

But when he was asked to relinquish all that he had, he did so without hesitation. Abraham did so because God had asked him to share his wealth and time in a distant land — a place where his talents could be best used to create something even grander than material wealth.

Then God asked Abraham to take his son and go out to the mount — to the place that would become

Jerusalem — to offer his son as a sacrifice. Even then, Abraham was willing to offer the life of his own loins, the only son he had that would carry on his name. But God would say, "Abraham, no. I was just testing. I just wanted to see if you were able to share even the best you had."

I think of a man down the line from Abraham: Joseph, the wondrous son of Jacob. He was the object of his brothers' jealousy. They imprisoned him in a cistern with the intent of murdering him. Just as they were to kill him, they decided instead to sell him off as a slave into Egypt, where he endured much hardship.

But his path led him to much wealth, for he became the right-hand man of the Pharaoh. It was then that his brothers came to Egypt seeking food in a time of want. And what did Joseph do? He shared what he had with his brothers, he sent for his father, and together, they became one of the wealthiest families in Egypt.

I think too of another great man some 400 years later. His name was Moses. Moses was Pharaoh's grandson by adoption, but he gave up that position to help his own Israelite people. He went to Pharaoh time and time again, asking him to allow them to go back to their homeland.

He not only risked the anger of the Pharaoh, he risked the resentment of his own people. For 40 years Moses endured this. He shared what he had from God with them, and oftentimes he was treated very shamefully.

I think, too, of a great king whose name was David. He had conquered his enemies, built up Jerusalem and made Israel the most powerful nation in that part of the world. Yet, more than anything else, he wanted not to acquire more houses and land, but rather to build a temple to God.

He wanted to show Yahweh that he loved him with all of his heart. Yet Yahweh would say to him, "It is not my plan that you do this. I have reserved this for your son Solomon." So David, in his own great, wondrous love, shared his dream and let his son perform this work.

The Old Testament is not the only place where I found men and women willing to do wondrous things for God by sharing their time, their talents and their resources.

The New Testament is filled with the likes of Mary, that wonderful maiden of Nazareth, and her husband Joseph. They had their own dreams of what their life would be, including the children they would have and the things they would build together.

But such was not to be. God said to Mary that she was to give birth to the holy one of God. Her task was not to populate the human family, but to work with God to bring about a divine Son.

Mary endured ridicule for being pregnant and unmarried. Once she and Joseph were married, she had to leave the comfort and security of Nazareth on a long journey to Bethlehem, not knowing where the child would be born. She ended up giving birth to him in a stable.

Mary and Joseph then went off into Egypt, the very land from which their forefathers had escaped. They gave up their own ideas and will in order to do what God asked of them.

I think of that other wondrous man who was alive during Jesus' time, John the Baptist. God made it known to him that he would be the ambassador of the new Messiah. To accomplish this, John gave up the comfort of living with his parents, and lived out in the desert eating locusts and wild honey, and wearing animal furs to keep warm. He would be ridiculed at times. Eventually he would be imprisoned and beheaded. He shared even his life with God.

There were also more ordinary men, like the brothers Peter and Andrew, James and John. They left their fishing businesses because Jesus said to them, "I will make you fishers of men rather than of fish from the Sea of Galilee." They gave up all the things that a young, ambitious person would treasure in order to be partners and follow Christ.

We can also look at a man like Paul. He had been selected by the high priest to imprison wayward Jews. He was looked upon and admired. After that day he lay blinded on the road to Damascus, he knew that he would have to share everything he had. He had to become all things to all men, that he might share with them the wonderment of Christ. So it would be until, at last, he gave his life outside the walls of the City of Rome.

The early Christians as related by Saint Luke held all things in common so that no one would be without.

They would sell their farms or whatever possessions
they had and give the proceeds to the Apostles who,
in turn, would share it with all of the people in need.

As I read about these heroes in the sacred scriptures, I thought to myself, this is wonderful! When you
give away, you get so much in return. Sharing is
indeed the way of God.

Over the years, these figures became my heroes.
They were the models for my life. They took my teenage
heart — which, at the time, was so full of self-interest —
and they enlarged it in such a way that "self" would
never be good enough. I had to follow them. I had to
leave myself and become like them, especially like
Christ. My small little world was being changed into a
giant world that would embrace all of God's family.

That October day in 1950, when I left the place
where I was born and raised and headed for the uncertain future of Appalachia, I talked to Jesus all the way.

I had one major prayer: "Please Lord, let me share
with all the people I shall meet in this land, all the
gifts and strengths I have. Please Lord, make me
always a giver. I don't have much now. Please keep it
that way. Maybe what you said in the scriptures is true.
It is more blessed to give than to receive. You said,
'Learn of me for I am meek and humble of heart.' You
emptied yourself and took on the form of a slave. And
surely greater love than this no one has, that he would
lay down his life for his friends."

Now 50 years have passed since that October day.
Has the prayer been answered? Oh, there is no question

that my journey of 50 years has generated a great deal of attention and resulted in much change, hopefully for the better.

The question I have always to ask myself is, "What caused the change? What brought about such an outpouring of giving?

"Was it the longevity of 50 years sticking to the task? Was it all the programs that I and my CAP family have worked so diligently to promote?

"Was it organization, and the gathering together of people who knew their unique roles and tasks in the challenge placed before them? Was it publicity?"

I'm sure all of these things have played a role. But I believe that it has been love that has brought about the change. A love patterned after the scripture heroes, and especially after the love of Christ.

Without question, it is that love, that willingness to share, and that statement before God that you can have what I have, that keeps us going.

When I came to the mountains 50 years ago, I had to care for an area as large as the State of Rhode Island. For every thousand people who lived in this area, there was only one Catholic.

My work was to be evangelical in nature, to purchase land and build churches. It was also to help the poor in one of the poorest places in America. Yet, as I looked at my challenge, I had no money, I had no great skills, I was very young, and I was looked upon as an outsider because of my Catholic faith.

I think CAP's success began the day the first family knocked on my door at Berea and asked for help. They were not Catholic. They wouldn't even call me "Father." I saw the troubles they were facing, and my sharing heart went out to them. I shared what little I had and promised more.

I think also that CAP's success was manifest in a widow who came to me one day. She lived on the banks of the North Fork of the Kentucky River at a little place called Saint Helens in Lee County. She was in poor health and had no way to care for her three daughters. She wanted to know if I could find a home for her children.

I got her a place to stay and found a Catholic orphanage at St. Aloysius in Cincinnati. The children were cared for there, and eventually were reunited with their mother once she got better.

Looking back, I think the uncertainty of that request to St. Aloysius — hoping they'd say yes — was one of the ingredients for building success.

I think success also came because I started a camp for young children. I probably shouldn't have pursued that uncertain venture, given the other requests I had from my church. After all, I was supposed to be building churches. Instead, I wanted to benefit the children and I felt that by starting a camp, I was doing something special for these little people of God.

An amazing thing began happening. CAP was getting help and support that I had never thought about, and had no reason to expect. CAP was sharing and, as a result, things were happening.

Sure, there were times when I was frustrated.

Why didn't my church give more support to me? Why didn't the Commonwealth of Kentucky — that I loved so much and that had such a great history of doing good – turn its attentions to the Appalachian area, the most depressed area they had? Why didn't the people who gave to other charities care about the poorest, most neglected part of America?

I was frustrated with God, too. He has power and influence. Why didn't he get more people motivated about the poverty of Appalachia? Couldn't he get people to remember CAP in their wills or set up a foundation or endowment? Couldn't he get those people who have so much to share with those who have so little?

Today, years later, I still get frustrated with God. As I go on in my foolishness, complaining, the Lord comes to me and asks me to quell my complaints.

The Lord says to me, "Look where you are. After just one year here, you had people coming and volunteering. And that was only after one year." The Lord continues, "Look at all the volunteers who have come in the years since then. CAP grew because you never ceased to share.

"The early volunteers helped the poor; only a portion of their time was used for building a church. Every donation you received – be it food, clothing, money or building materials – was used to help those in need, even though you might have needed them to build another house of worship for me.

"CAP helps people of every faith, not just your own. CAP helps even those who have no faith, those who are still searching. You reach out to them because they were in need. Many times, others wouldn't even bother to listen to them, much less help them.

"Oftentimes, those you help don't even realize the help came from you.

"Look at the program you started at CAP many years ago. You asked CAP to share its money by giving grants to other groups and organizations, rather than using them for your own projects. You took chances, but you did so because there was a need.

Then the Lord changes the subject and turns to me. He asks me, "How do you feel?"

I say to him, "You know that I am just getting over the worst cold and flu that I have ever had in my life."

"How about your eyes?"

"Well, they're not as good as they used to be. I have to keep going to the doctor for laser treatments."

"How about your knee that you had replaced, and the arthritis that makes it difficult for you to walk? I don't hear you complaining. What goes on in that white-haired head of yours?"

I say to the Lord, "You know what goes on, Lord. I give the pain and the discouragement to you, so that you can help the poor and move others to help them as well."

"So you share your sufferings with the poor and with me?" the Lord says. "Don't you understand that that is why you have brought about so many changes? You have shared the best you have, which is your suffering and your uncertainties. In the years ahead I will ask you to give much more. Without a doubt, the best you can give for me still lies ahead."

Then the Lord says a strange thing. "Are you happy? Does joy fill your day?"

"Yes, Lord, when day ends and bed is near, I look up there where I know you are and I still have the prayer I had that first day 50 years ago, when I drove down to Appalachia. 'Please Lord, let me share with all the people I shall meet in this land, all the gifts and strengths that I have. Please Lord, make me always be a giver.' Lord, here lies my happiness, my joy. Sharing is the way in which I find happiness."

By this time it's late and pen and paper have been laid aside.

"There is one thing more I want to say," says the Lord. "I want to thank you for the things you do for people who are not poor. You always ask them to give themselves and their resources to help someone else, and that is such a blessing. Your message of sharing has not only helped the poor, it has affected those who are well-off as well.

"In sharing their material resources, they are going to find more peace and happiness than they ever could holding onto them. You have brought joy to them as well as hope to the poor."

I think about these things in a moment of quiet. Then I simply say, "Thank you, Lord. Please help me, though. You know how frail and weak I am, and how quickly I complain and feel sorry for myself."

By this time, I have headed off to my bed. My prayers are now ended. I take out my book on Christian Heroes and I read about Francis Xavier, that wonderful missionary from Spain. He spent his life serving God.

As I read his story, I notice that not once in the last 25 years of his life did he get what he really wanted or accomplish those things on which he had set his heart. He had to accept what God asked of him.

Yet, he was still one of the greatest Christian heroes. He profoundly changed the 16th century.

I close the book and put it aside. "Francis," I say, "I want to be like you. I always want to share and change because of what God wants, just as you did."

Then a quiet little voice comes back. Francis says to me, "Just say each day, my dear friend, what our lady said to the archangel that day in Nazareth: 'Behold the handmaid of the Lord. Be it done to me according to thy word.' Say that every day, and you will always share."

"Thank you, dear Francis." I say. "Have a good night."

I turn out the light. Another day has been shared with God. A day of love.

Chapter 4 The Love of Home

For two weeks in January I went to Florida for a vacation. My brother Stanley, who had retired from his carpentry work the first day of January, kindly agreed to drive me to Florida and back.

During our drive, we had time to talk and relive old memories. Stanley is 14 years younger than I, but so many of our memories center on the same place — the home in which we grew up.

It was a very blessed place. As the world appraises houses, it was not much — an old frame house anchored on ten acres of rolling hills. Four rooms and a large kitchen were on the first floor. An attic covered the house, and there we seven boys shared a bedroom. The four girls and my parents had the first floor.

A coal-burning furnace backed up by a large coal bin occupied the basement. There were shelves down there that featured my mother's canning efforts.

The front yard was supposed to be a well-cut grassy place, and it did feature the flower beds my mother had placed there. But much to my mother's great dismay, we had made it all into a ballfield. The neighbors kindly lent their yard to complete our ball-field and outfield.

We did have a wondrous back porch. The pump that drew water from the well was there. We had our barn, our stall for the cow, and a field for our back yard. The pig pen and chicken coop completed the scene.

Oh yes, there was also an outhouse with a well-trodden path leading to it.

In the back fields was our pasture, where you could find the fruit trees, a large garden and the hay field. We also had a woodland where we built our forts and castles.

Stan and I, though 14 years apart, had the same memories. Our house was a place of security. It was a place of work. It brought us so much pleasure. We usually ran the last distance as we came home from school.

In a very real sense, we hated to leave the house. Instead, we invited all the neighboring kids to come and be a part of all activities there. Our home was the place where we wanted to be.

By all accounts we lived out in the country in a substandard house, yet we were happy. We laughed, we cried and, at times, we fought. At mealtime, we took time to pray. And before we went to bed at night, my mother handed out the treats after we said our night prayers.

Both Stan and I agreed that our home was the most wonderful place that we ever experienced. It was a place of love, where Mother and Father showed the way. It was a place where we learned to share and work together for the good of all.

The house has long since been torn down. A new highway was needed, and new stores along its course. Where our house once stood, a parking lot now stands. But that house with its lilac bush, its ballfields, the cistern on the back porch, the coal-burning stove that cooked all of our meals, and even the outhouse, was truly a comfort that is indelibly still in our minds. It will remain there until death steals away our memories.

Truly for me there was no place like home.

When I came to the mountains of Appalachia 50 years ago, I saw so many houses that were much worse from the physical standpoint than the one in which I had grown up. Oftentimes there were just one or two rooms.

I had to be awfully careful when I walked in the houses of some of these poor folks. The floors in many places had given away. You could see the holes in the roof at times that allowed the rain to ruin so much that was inside. The walls never had any insulation in them, nor did the roofs. Frequently, the outside walls were no more than an inch thick, just rough oak nailed together.

A crude wood-burning fireplace or stove tried desperately to drive away the cold and the dampness. A naked light bulb hanging from a cord sought to dispel the darkness. Junk of all kinds plagued the yard. Everything that no longer worked surrounded the house.

But as full of blight as these scenes were, the worst was that there was no smiling, no laughter, to drive away the gloom. You simply hung on. You didn't dance, you didn't jump, you didn't sing with joy. Happiness was a stranger. These homes were places that stilled any dreaming and took away hope.

At times I had to take children out of these homes. These children were frequently dying of pneumonia and various other illnesses. I took others to orphanages when parents had died or were no longer able to care for them.

Since then, I've taken children to camps where dreams are born and instilled in them. I've taken them to Bible schools, where hope and love are found in the trial of Bethlehem. I've taken them to child development centers where learning was found to be a joy and not a curse.

It was one of my strongest desires and convictions that I was in these mountains not only to build houses for God's Son, but also to build houses for the other children of God who had so little of their own. I could not peacefully live in a house where comforts were everywhere and see so many of my brothers and sisters in Christ suffer so much because they had no worthy place to live.

As soon as I could, I began to call out to my family and friends to come down and help me. "Bring your hammer and your saw, your shovel and your paintbrush!" I told them. "Let us turn these rundown buildings into homes of light and warmth and peace."

For 50 years, my friends of church and CAP have worked unceasingly to change the face of our Appalachian hills.

Besides the volunteers, I had to get materials to repair these hurting houses. I went to lumber dealers, sash and door companies, and manufacturers of shingles, carpet, tile, and paint. I was shocked and surprised to hear how many of them said, "Yes." I cannot adequately express the depth of gratitude I feel for these companies. I only wish they could walk the valleys and hills with me and enter a house now filled with smiles, and with laughter ringing from the walls.

Without these companies, we at CAP would never have had the success that has crowned our 50 years of labor. So generous have they been that I had to rent warehouses to store these materials until they could be adequately used.

It was not long before many others who served the poor discovered our warehouses. They marveled at the variety and quantity of the materials we had gathered. "Would it be possible," they asked, half ashamed, "if we could get some of your materials so that we too could help the poor?"

And we said to them, "Of course you may!" Almost every day we have charitable groups coming to these warehouses with pick-up trucks to haul things away. Because of this, there will be better houses in counties that we know we cannot reach ourselves.

The warehouses are like a divine magnet drawing so many good groups to us. Our efforts to help the poor have been multiplied a hundred-fold by these wonderful people. We are but servants — come and share in this work. Take and build, and together we can change the face of Appalachia.

I marvel at the people who come to the warehouses. A minister came just the other day and asked if he could have siding. He didn't want it just to help the little church that he served, but also to improve the houses of some the poorest members of his congregation.

There was a group that came from Olive Hill. They were remodeling a building to make a community center — Sarah's Place they called it. They asked if they could have some doors and windows. Once again, I assured them that it was indeed possible and I helped them to load their truck.

I think too of other groups that do all sorts of works. In fact, in one week alone, we shared four truckloads of windows and doors with them so that they could spread out over five counties that they served – counties that we were not able to serve ourselves.

I have even seen private individuals come. Not so long ago, I was so impressed by a lady who came asking for a couch. Lightening had come through the window during a storm and burned up her couch. Thankfully, they were able to put out the fire before anything worse happened. We loaded the couch onto her truck – and a chair to go with it.

I also remember a gentleman who had received publicity because his group had done a great deal to improve housing for the poor. He came to me and asked, "Did you see the television spot?" to which I replied, "Yes."

"I am so ashamed to come here because of that," said he.

"Why?" I asked.

"I was given the credit for all of it," he replied. "You were the one who gave me the materials. You were the one who gave me the supplies. Without you, I couldn't have done it and you weren't mentioned in the story at all."

"That isn't necessary," I said. "It isn't for us that we are working, but for the poor — and that is what we take pride in. We are grateful to you for making it come about."

So many people have been impressed by our efforts. They have come forward offering their time and help – a thing they never would have done, had it not been for the examples they saw at our warehouses.

In recent years, we have gone beyond the repair and the remodeling of homes. I remember one day, a man up in Martin County came to me and said, "Can you come to my house and see if you can do something to help us?"

He had five children, and they lived in a rickety three-room house with a swing inside the front porch.

As I went through the house, I saw that there was no insulation, the wiring was so substandard it could not be used, the walls and roof leaked, and the floors sagged. I said to them quite simply that there was no way that we could repair this house and make it something worthwhile. What they really needed was a new home.

The man sighed. "How can I ever get that?"

To which I replied, "We will help."

I contacted a group from Louisville. We supplied the materials they needed and, with labor from the group and from the family itself, we built them a new home. It was amazing to see the joy and happiness that came. The children ran out the door and jumped on the porch and everyone laughed and cried.

We simply have to go into the business of helping folks like these build new houses. Sometimes families are able to furnish some of the money. Other times they are willing to commit themselves to paying off part of it. Either way, the families are deeply involved.

We are trying desperately in our housing programs at CAP to not only repair older homes but also dedicate our efforts to building new ones. Our goal this coming year is to remodel at least 105 homes and to construct 25 new ones.

At times these new houses have been built on simple plots of land that these people have been able to acquire. At other times we have built small communities. In fact, we built one community of 15 houses, with streets and yards for the people to enjoy. In another area we put up a section of 20 houses.

In these cases, we buy the tract of land, but we always buy judiciously and get a reduced price.

One day I was at a meeting of the Kentucky Appalachian Regional Commission. The commission was set up by our governor, and I am a member. We were meeting in Pikeville and, during a break in the morning session, a gentleman came up to me and asked, "Don't you remember me, Father Beiting?"

"I'm afraid I don't," I said.

He went on to say that he was one of my volunteers from over 30 years ago. He had come down from Yale University for a year to help build. "Now I'm a architect," he said. "I made up my mind in the days I was helping you that I would come back to these mountains to do something to improve its looks and build beautiful things."

I almost had to cry as he said this. I realized that his conviction had taken root over 30 years ago.

So sure was he of this mission, he had said to his fiancée that if she wanted to be his wife, the mountains of Eastern Kentucky would be where they would live. They have been here ever since and have raised their children here.

The story of building, of course, is still unfolding. Each spring, nearly 250 college students from all over the United States come to help us. Most of their work is involved in repairing houses and getting to know the people for whom they are working, and seeing the challenge that still remains.

I simply have to sit back and wait for the years to roll by, because I know many of these students will perform vital work in Eastern Kentucky in the years ahead. I'm sure that of the 250 that will come this spring, many will return.

But even if they don't, what we have done is to make them conscious of the needs of the poor. They will respond in many ways in their own communities and throughout the world. Many of them join up with

Habitat for Humanity, not only here in the United
States but also in foreign countries.

All that will begin on the day they arrive in
Appalachia. We show them the challenge, work with
them, give them ideas, nudge them toward the
answers, and show them how much they are needed.

Some days when I'm in a car with nowhere in particular to go, I simply drive past many of the homes we
have repaired or built. I don't just follow the major
roads but go back into the hollows and into the hills.
It is there that you see the work that has been done.

I was in a meeting not so long ago in Martin
County. The young man in charge of economic development for the county said that when he was at the
University of Kentucky, he had to write a paper about
someone who challenged his life and had done much
for the area in which he had lived.

He said, "I wrote about you, Father Beiting. I
called you the 'Preacher Man of Appalachia.' I'm so
proud of what you have done and the homes you have
fixed up, and all the other things you have made come
about."

This is part of what we have been trying to do
over the years. We have been sincerely at work — not
only with the people of Appalachia, asking them to
improve their housing in their own regard, but also
asking them to help others.

We have challenged the college students and the
churches. We have also said a great deal to the people
who live in these houses.

We've told them, "This house is but a shell — a place of brick and mortar, wood and nails. Making it a place of joy and excitement will be up to you. You will have to bring in that spirit with love and dedication and discipline, and all the other things that make happiness. And when you see the children's eyes light, when you see them willing to give up a Saturday to go out and help a neighbor, you know you've really done something."

I guess one of the great things that I would have done, had I been there in Christ's time, would have been to build him a house so that he could have been born there instead of in a stable.

Yet what He tells me each day is that I have done that. I have built Him a house — by building homes for the smallest of His brethren.

I get home after a day in which I have been involved either in warehousing, or helping with construction, or thanking donors, or meeting with volunteers. I go out to the back porch with the wood-burning stove, and make a warm spot for myself in the late evening.

And I say to God, "I want to thank You for what You have inspired me to do — for what You have asked me to do. The things we have been doing here to create homes are so important. A home gives people security. It gives them a chance to dream. It gives them the opportunity to look at tomorrow with some sense of hope. I want you to know, Lord, that I am so grateful.

I'm thankful that You have given me the help I need to unload trucks, to store things in warehouses and load them up again. I'm grateful that I can still run a saw. I can still take up a hammer and nail and make the metal ring."

The Lord says to me, "You have so much to overcome in your imperfection. And yet I am encouraged by your efforts, and I will give you my grace to make you strong and never feel discouraged or overwhelmed.

"All I ask is that you give Me yourself and, if you do that, nothing less than good will come about. I'm still very much a part of the program."

I finish my conversation with the Lord and bid Him good night with my evening prayer. I close the breviary, put it on my desk, and head for my bedroom. There on the nightstand, as always, is my book of Christian Heroes.

The one I read about tonight is one of the most special people that God has ever made. He was a carpenter. He spent his life helping people build houses and build homes. His name, of course, was Joseph.

I say to Joseph, "I am so grateful that I have come from a heritage of carpenters. My great-grandfather, my grandfather, and my father were all carpenters. So was my brother Stanley. I hope that I have used what they taught me to build houses for the poor.

"Joseph, will you pray for me that I may continue to have the opportunity to shelter the needy and give comfort to the old? Housing is such important work and, Joseph, we need to build. Will you help me?"

I close the book and turn out the light and turn over. And Joseph says simply to me, "Just do what the Lord asks. I, myself, had revelations from the Lord in a dream, and I was willing to do what he asked. So, when the inspiration comes to you to reach out and build another house, to repair another place, to build another ramp, please do it. Don't worry about the costs. Don't worry about the difficulties. Just do it."

And I say, "Thank you Joseph. I will not be quiet. I will not be still.

"I will make the hammer ring and the saw sing. I will build. I will not let the plain be empty and naked. Goodnight, and thank you for all the nice things you do for me."

Chapter 5 The Love of Health

I have just returned from the February board meeting of Pikeville College. I am on the Board of Trustees of this very fine institution. We heard a report from the College of Osteopathic Medicine by its dean, John Strosnider.

John's school is just in its third year, but even now, its enrollment and success are far beyond what we had hoped for when we began this program. As I listened to a report filled with hope and expectation, I felt so satisfied.

It was a little over four years ago that I was invited to the governor's house in Frankfort, our state capital. CAP, together with a number of other institutions, was asked if we would pledge some financial assistance to this new college about to begin. It was hoped that the College of Osteopathic Medicine would be a great part of Appalachia. Today, the school has become a reality.

The students who attend this school are now serving internships in 13 hospitals in Kentucky's and West Virginia's Appalachian counties.

This all bodes very, very well for the mountains. For, the likelihood of medical students staying on here is much greater when they serve the Appalachian area itself and are applauded and appreciated for their efforts.

At CAP a few years back, we sat down and went over the major problems of Appalachia. Health care was one of the most vital. We thought and prayed over the problem. Many of the band-aid approaches so many charities were using, while good in themselves, would never seriously change the condition of health in our area.

We at CAP are dedicated as this new millennium begins to seek permanent answers. There can never be a permanent solution without adequate professional healers. Only when we have the proper number of doctors will we truly attack the problem of poor health. We knew then that a school of medicine in one of our Appalachian colleges would be ideal.

I was especially delighted to get a request from the son of two of our former volunteers. He asked me to write a recommendation for him for the Osteopathic College at Pikeville. His parents had married after meeting each other here through their volunteer work.

His father, Moe, is now one of CAP's Vice Presidents and his mother is a very fine nurse. I was so pleased to get the son's request. The parents' spirit of service has spread to the new generation.

Love is at work and it will not be stopped. Love is too powerful an element. It shall overcome.

I am home now from the meeting and it is night. Once again, I am out on my little enclosed porch. The wood-burning fireplace makes it comfortable on a winter night. I like this place. I am alone out here. There are no distractions so it is a wonderful place to meditate.

I have seen so much in these past 50 years, it has kindled in me a great love for my mountain people. I have found that love comes more powerfully when you see someone suffer. And I have seen the people of Appalachia suffer from poor health from those very first days.

I remember a Sunday when I was traveling from my church in Berea to the chapel down in Mt. Vernon. I had limited time to make the journey. There, crouched by the side of the road on a cold winter Sunday morning, was an old man with a cane. I doubled back and asked, "Sir, what is the matter?"

He replied, "I'm so sick I can't stand. I crawled out of the house to come out to the road in the hope that someone would stop and pick me up and take me to the hospital." But no one had.

So I helped him into my car, turned around, and raced back to Berea to the hospital.

His life was probably saved that Sunday morning. But the memory of him sitting there on the side of the road in the middle of the cold winter was something I can't forget.

I remember the little boy at Sandgap. When I came to see him, his parents lived in an old one-room garage. A naked bulb hanging from the ceiling gave them what light they had.

The child's skin was blue. I said to his parents, "This boy is very ill."

They said, "We know. He's burning up. We put wet rags on his head but he keeps getting hot again."

I had them bundle the boy up and get into my car, for they did not have one. We went down the mountain until we got to the hospital. A couple more hours and the boy would not have lived.

I remember an old lady who lived in a trailer in Martin County, KY. We sat out on her porch for a while. She told me how much she loved me — although she had not ever met me before.

She loved me because, thanks to you, our CAP workers were able to do much to make her feel better. They had brought her medicine from the store, they had taken her to a doctor, they had sat by her side and simply been there.

She reached out her gnarled and twisted hands and took mine. She said, "I shall pray for you every day so that you can continue to do good for people like me."

I remember another Saturday more than 30 years ago. I was up in the mountains having mass and instructing the Catholic children in Jackson County. The children told me of a lady who was dying. So, on my way back I stopped at her house. It was a three-room shed, home to five children and a mother and father.

The mother was in bed, dying of cancer. It was such a sad sight. The children didn't laugh or cry. The husband sat there perplexed, not knowing what to do. So I gave him some money to get some medicine for his wife.

I stopped by the next three Saturdays to see how they were doing, only to realize that the woman was getting weaker each time I came. By the fourth Saturday, she had passed away.

For the last 35 years, her husband has sent donations to me for CAP. He explains, "You were the only one to stop and give. I belong to a lodge and nobody came to see me. I belong to a church and no one came to see me. And, here you were, a stranger, who came by. You gave us help and you prayed and we will never forget."

I think back on all the children I have seen at our camps since I opened the first one in 1957. I was so shocked to see that even though they'd not reached their teens, their teeth were nearly gone. Their teeth had decayed from lack of care and an improper diet.

I have seen so many over the years who didn't have or know about a proper diet. They ate junk food. They didn't have any realization that this type of food was not healthy and that they would pay a terrible price in years to come.

I have seen the sick in their little trailers and their sheds and I have held their hands and prayed with them as they died. I hoped that my prayers would bless them as they departed from this terrible place to a much better world.

It's 10 o'clock and I am tired. Besides the meeting earlier in the day, I have traveled over 250 miles.

Sadness overwhelms me from these and countless other memories.

In my exhaustion, I cry out to God, "Why, Lord, why is it that the poor suffer so much? Why doesn't the richest nation on earth hear their cries and see their misery? Must we always be concerned only with the crowded, the urban areas? They have so much more medical care. Why can't they see the isolation of our mountains and the hurt that results from it?

"These people are my family, Lord. I see my mother and father in many of them. They lie there helpless and with no one to come to their aid.

"I see others that are younger and like brother and sister to me. The little ones could be my own children if I had them. Lord, I care so deeply for them. Can't you do better and do it soon? Can't you do something to change the heart and mind of our people so that this misery does not have to keep growing?"

I stop after a while. I am tired even of complaining. So I am silent. And in the quiet, a voice can be heard — Jesus himself.

"Why do you always place the blame on Me for the suffering of your people? Each day you read the scriptures. Did I not heal the sick? What about the lady with the flow of blood who had suffered so much over 12 years? She simply touched My garment and she was well.

"Don't you remember the lepers who were so possessed with sores and illness that they were an outcast to all people? I made them whole. You read about the blind who could not see, and how I touched their eyes with spittle from My lips and how they saw again. And you saw the paralyzed people – people who had to be brought in by cots and lowered down through the roof of the house where I was — and how I touched them and they picked up their pallets and walked away, singing and dancing.

"I even drove devils out of the possessed. They were well again and they went forth speaking of the goodness of God. And at times I even raised the dead – those that had died of illness. The centurion came to me and asked if I would heal his servant. I said but a word and the boy was healed.

"Do you remember the widow of Nain? They were taking her only son out to the cemetery and I simply said, 'Young man, I say to you, arise.'

"How can you say to me, 'Can you not heal?' Or do you think I love your generation less and with less intensity than the generation with whom I lived? Let me assure you that I care for every one of your sick and dying. I cry for them as much as I did for Lazarus when he was in the tomb and I was told that he was dead.

"What you have to realize is that my love for your people manifests itself differently than when I walked the earth. Back then, I could go about, touch people, and immediate results would come about. Don't you realize that I have gone back to heaven and my activity is of a different nature? Don't you realize that I have made you and all your people partners with me, caring for the sick?

"My power is still there, but it has to work through you and the rest of my brethren. What you must understand is that there is a partnership in healing. I'm not going to walk the earth and touch and use spittle and all the other things I once did. I'm now going to use you and others like you, and together we are going to be the medical team.

"You have to ask yourself if you have been a faithful partner with me. Have you carried and shared the task?"

Oh, I hate it when he talks like that to me. He always comes up with the truth, and that hurts.

"Oh Lord," I say, "I just don't think deeply enough. I try to escape. It's always easier to blame someone else than to look at my own being."

"You still have a long way to go" says the Lord, "but you and your CAP family have been partners with me in so many ways. I wonder if you remember all of them? Even when you first came to the mountains, you were bringing comfort to the sick by visiting them and letting them know that they were important and loved.

"Look at the tens of thousands of visits your CAP family has made to the homebound. They receive at times more benefits from these visits than from the medicine itself.

"As you established the schools and camps, you and your staff of volunteers always emphasized the importance of good eating as a way to prevent illness. The friendly talks that the staff had with these children who admired them made a great impression. Good eating lifestyles were established and would pay dividends in the future.

"Don't you remember all of these things? In just the last couple of years CAP has assigned qualified personnel to visit public schools in the Appalachian area and work with the nurses there to show the children how important it is to take preventive measures that prevent illness and disease.

"You are partners with me in preventing illness. This is a very important step. It certainly is one that will have greater impact than caring for the people after they are already sick."

The Lord continues, "You know how isolated the people of Appalachia are — especially the elderly when sickness and disease enter their homes at a relatively early age. There is no public transportation and frequently, these elderly are alone. Their families had to move away to secure employment.

"But for many years now, your people have taken countless thousands of the elderly to hospitals, doctors and clinics. You have taken these elderly and made them family with you and with me. You have been an instrument of health, and I hope you don't forget that.

"I also admire," the Lord says, "how your CAP family has become involved in obtaining prescription drugs. You have made it possible for so many to get the proper medicine they need which they otherwise couldn't afford. Your volunteers and employees go out every day, working with the people, the doctors and the pharmacies. Help comes to them which never would have found its way. Healing takes place because you were a partner with me.

"It was my grace that motivated people who never come to Appalachia but simply get your letters in the mail to answer with the donations that enable you to do these things.

"Don't you realize how many letters they get in a day's time? Yet when they pick yours to answer, do you think it was not because I prompted them?

"You always think that someone should do this or that. It is my plan that a partnership be formed between all of you on earth and Myself. We can create a team that can bring health to all that suffer. It is not a task that will be accomplished today and the victory won. But if you have the vision and the realization that I am at your side, hoarding the strength necessary for success, then you will understand how big a part you can play in the healing of My people.

"You forget the past successes so easily. You get so involved with what still has to be done. Don't be so angry or impatient. Do all that you can today, and I can make it grow more than you'll ever realize as the days go on. You plant and cultivate. I will get the increase."

"Lord" I say, "You are so wise. I hate to hear You at times. You always get to the bottom of things. But when You finish speaking, I am more determined than ever to be Your partner. Yell at me whenever You want. Somehow I will listen."

The door opens in the little glass porch. One of the volunteers comes in and hands me the telephone. My sister-in-law Rose Beiting is on the line. She tells me that her mother died a few hours before. Could I come up to Northern Kentucky on Wednesday to have her funeral?

Rose's mother was a lady in her nineties, a widow for a dozen years or more. The last year or so she had been in a nursing home. She had suffered much in the last months, but she wanted to offer her sufferings to God. She felt she could get much good out of that and give much good to others.

One morning she asked the nurse if she could call a priest. She had already been anointed and so the nurse asked why. Her response was that she wanted a priest to come and pray with her. The nurses notified her family and they quickly came to her and they prayed with her. They sat around the bed and just simply prayed the rosary and other wonderful prayers.

I felt so proud of them when I heard what they had done. Prayer and talking about our Savior is one of the most important things we can do to help the sick. We have to prepare them for meeting the greatest hero of all. Only He can truly make them well.

We have to see the whole person – the soul as well as the body. We must never forget this. I have seen people at death's door suffering terribly, but there are smiles on their faces because they have been freed from their sin and united to God. Peace is their reward.

This I think about as I remember the past. Many of these poor people I've written about were really comforted by the prayers we said, the hands we held, and the assurance that we would never let God alone. We would keep praying to Him so that they would be helped.

That was the case with Rose's mother. What a tremendous help comes to the soul and spirit when you let people know that they are loved and cared for, and that God is there to welcome and help them, not to condemn and punish.

By now it is after 11 p.m. I retire to bed and pick up my wonderful book on Christian Heroes.

The friend that I read about tonight is Mother Teresa, a wonderful lady who had been involved with so much healing all over the world, even here. I helped her sisters come to Appalachia. They now work in the Jenkins area in Letcher County.

"Dear Mother," I ask, "how can I do the wonderful work you did? How can I help the sick as you have?"

"My son," she says, "I followed the advice of Saint Augustine. He said to work as if everything depended upon you, and pray as if everything depended upon God.

"Do what you can and do it consistently and then pray to God. I assure you that He will care for the sick more than all of the hospitals and clinics of the world."

I turn out the light and settle down for the next day. "Lord," I say, "thank You for giving me such a wonderful example as Mother Teresa. Tomorrow I shall be renewed. I shall go on. I shall never stop loving, Lord. I shall do my part and never get tired of doing good, especially to these, the most needy of your children. Good night, Lord."

Chapter 6   The Love of Education

When time allows, I like to sit in a quiet place and remember days gone by. I am doing this now in a strange place for a man of the mountains. I'm in a hotel room in Fort Lauderdale, FL.

I am here for a couple of days to give talks about the work you support through CAP. I have been on the radio and in newspapers. I have also signed copies of my latest books and talked to some of our local donors. It has been a rewarding, if busy, day. Now in the quiet of the hotel room, I have time to think.

My mind turns to one of the most important challenges of the new millennium in Appalachia: education.

I think of my own education. I spent many years as a student, earning degrees in a number of colleges and universities. In recent years, I have been given several honorary doctorates for the work I have done to help the poor — especially in the work of education.

When did I get my love of education? When did it become such a joy?

Of course, I had some wonderful teachers from grade school on. But I think the teacher I owe the most to was my grandfather. He never got a chance to

go to high school. As the oldest in his family, he was
taught the carpenter trade. He became an expert
at it.

But he became much more as well. He was mysti-
fied by what he didn't know, and when he didn't know
the answers, he read. He never stopped reading. He
built knowledge upon knowledge until it became a
grand edifice. History was one of his favorite topics,
but he also had a deep love for mathematics.

Being his oldest grandchild, I was his helper as he
planted and gardened on our small farm. I also helped
him with his carpentry work, repairing the church and
helping to build a house for one of my uncles. My
grandfather always insisted that we walk to these jobs
sites, which were often two miles from home. During
these walks, he taught me so many things: history,
geometry, algebra and even trigonometry.

When we got home, he would often pull out books
and show me these things. Books opened a world of
wonder and promise. I couldn't help but see that he
loved knowledge.

I could see that he loved me, too. He wanted me
to experience the splendor of exploring the unknown.
He wanted me to have a deep and rich education.

From those days on, I knew that if I ever fell in
love, I would have to share knowledge with the ones
I loved. I'd have to open for them that hidden,
unknown world.

Love was truly a many-splendored thing, and
knowledge was one of the brightest stars in that splendor.

I owe my grandfather so very much. He loved education and he loved me, and the combination did wondrous things.

Before I came to the mountains in 1950, I taught in a Catholic high school. Strangely enough, the subjects I was assigned to teach were history and mathematics!

I always felt my grandfather was present in the classroom. Was I there because of love? Did I touch my students with love? I think he was reminding me that love was the only way that education could grow and be special.

My grandfather died 45 years ago, but I still remember the walks we took. And my love for the very heart of education is still there.

The very first effort I made in Appalachia to assist my mountain people was to set up a camp for children. My family helped me build the camp for about 50-60 children. It was on the banks of a lake near my church in Lancaster, KY.

When the kids came, we played ball, we shot arrows, we swam in the lake and rode on the boat. We fixed many a meal and bandaged many little hurts.

But I think the most important thing I did was gather the children around the campfire when evening came and tell them stories, painting pictures of what their futures could be. I showed them that there was no limit to what they could dream about and become. They could help build a better world. They could make a difference.

The key that would allow them to unlock this wonderful new world was education. I knew my stories succeeded in instilling something special in many young children at camp.

After that first summer, when the local school reopened in the fall, it wasn't long before the teachers asked me what I had done with the children. Their grades had improved and, even more special, they had a new zeal for school.

Over the years, many of these campers came back and thanked me for the change I had made in their lives. Most of them finished high school. Some went to college and graduated with distinction.

I often felt that my grandfather had been in the shadows of those campfires, even though death had taken him to a better world.

Another thing I did when I came to the mountains was to get volunteers to go with me and visit all the houses in a particular county. We wanted to know what the people saw as the greatest problem facing them.

Without fail, lack of education was in the top five of their concerns.

As we visited these houses, we saw so many bright and inquisitive youngsters. In them was a potential that needed to be tapped early — before pressure from older children convinced them that school and study were foolish things.

It was apparent that if love was to be put into practice, the education of these youngsters had to begin before elementary school.

We talked to their parents. They'd be okay if the three-, four-, and five-year-olds went to a place where they would learn and play with others. We told the parents we'd pick up the children in the morning and bring them home at the end of the day.

The parents trusted us with their precious children. They knew that genuine love prompted our concern. And the kids were glad to discover a world beyond their simple houses and yards.

In those days in the sixties, CAP started the first Child Development Programs in the area.

Just this month, we opened Genesis, a new Child Development Center, in an abandoned church in Lawrence County. Now this refurbished old church once again knows the laughter of children, as well as the holy quiet of children engrossed in learning a new skill.

CAP has taught their parents new skills, as well.

One evening a number of years ago, the wife of the governor of our state came to Renfro Valley to speak at a graduation ceremony for adults who had successfully completed their GED.

After the state's First Lady had given her talk, a graduate in her sixties stood up.

"I never finished grade school," she said, "and none of my kids did either. The mines had work then, and there were so many chores around our house. Going to school seemed like avoiding work and the chance to be happy. Now I'm old and I see the world has changed. I see how education is such an important part of it.

"I am so grateful you have given me the chance to learn, to read and to write," she continued. "I have said to my grandchildren, 'You will never be allowed to quit school. I'm going to see to it that you have the enthusiasm and the support to go every day. I will give you rewards when you come and show me your report cards. I want you to know that from your grandmother comes the greatest respect from education. The greatest approval I can give you is let you know that I want you to learn and be a better person.'"

There wasn't a dry eye when she sat down. CAP had changed a heart that was, in turn, going to change so many more.

At CAP, we are still turning to one and all in love, saying, "Let us learn together. Wonderful things are to be found around the corner."

Now I sit in my hotel room, looking out at the Florida night. I've enjoyed spending these few days in warmer weather. But I still miss my mountains, winter snow and cold and all.

I close my eyes, picturing their beauty. I think of the children and adults scattered throughout the hills and hollows, discovering, through education, the splendor of the unknown.

"Enjoy what has been done" says the Lord, "but don't get too pleased. The problem is not solved. The journey has just begun. I fear you will lose enthusiasm. Not everyone will share your vision and the way to carry it out. Of course, listen to criticism. It's the way to grow. But do not give up. I count on you more and more to bring me and my love into all the educational programs."

It is now midnight and I prepare for bed. I get out my special book on Christian Heroes, which I take with me on trips as well as read at home.

Tonight my hero is Father Don Bosco. He was an Italian who lived in the late 1880s, teaching reading, writing, arithmetic and vocational skills to abandoned and neglected children. His followers have taken his ideas to people in all parts of the world, especially to the poor in underdeveloped nations.

"Don Bosco" I say, "I sure admire you. Your work still continues more than 100 years after your death, all over the world. Will you pray for me and my CAP family that we can leave such a heritage here in the mountains of Appalachia?"

"Just do what the Lord tells you." he says. "Pray, don't get disheartened, and hold on to Him and His love, and your work in education will never die."

I close the book and turn out the lights.

"Lord, thank you for this day and the memories I've got. I shall not grow weary. I shall keep the light burning. With your help, I know it shall never go out.

"Good night, Lord. I'll see you back in Kentucky tomorrow."

Chapter 7 The Love of Worship

It is Saturday night. The week has been filled with so many worries and fears, I've wondered at times if truth and goodness have a chance.

I've seen disease make skeletons out of once strong and healthy people. My brother, who was an outstanding athlete in every category, is now so weak he just lies in the hospital bed. As I talked to him and prayed for him, he cried.

I visited one of my priest friends on another floor of the same hospital. He is much younger than I and was the chancellor of the Diocese of Covington. He now has cancer. I went to let him know that we had not forgotten him, that he was loved and that we prayed for him.

You could tell that he understood what I was saying although he was unable to respond. There he was lying on that bed, arms and legs stretched out, all sorts of tubes attached to him, unable to do anything for himself.

Next I traveled to a nursing home and visited three other priest friends of mine. I was saddened by their sense of failure. One after the other said to me, "We're nothing but old, infirm priests, unable to do any good for anybody."

I kept talking to them, saying, "What do you mean, you're doing nothing? You're doing what God has asked — you're suffering. You're doing things that you never would have wanted to do on your own. But because he has sent them to you, you're accepting them and offering them back to him with love.

"Don't you remember when our Lord said, 'Only when I was lifted up on the cross could I draw people to myself.'? He is asking you to come and be a part of him on this cross."

I was pleased to see the spark of hope come back into their eyes as I talked and prayed with them. They felt that perhaps they had a purpose, after all — and they had simply overlooked it for a while.

The same day, I presided at a funeral of the mother of my sister-in-law. It reminded me of other deaths in our family. It reminded me of all the teachers that I had, whose funerals I had attended — and women, priests and nuns, who had done so much to enliven education and bring excitement in my life.

It reminded me too of my own death, which simply can't be too far away.

On the other hand, I have seen much to renew precious hope this week.

I've been to senior citizens centers, carrying in food provided by my wonderful CAP family. As I came into their midst, the elders spoke so highly of the gratitude they felt for CAP and the work you and I have been doing to help sustain them.

I see their enthusiasm, and can't help but feel there is still hope strong in these hills.

The number of people like them is legion. So many want to help, but they need a way to do it – and so they come to me and to the CAP family.

I met a wonderful man who was so anxious to help. He is one of our volunteers from the farthest corner of Alaska. He really wants to be of great service and has offered himself to us.

He is ready to help with home repair, to see about maintenance, to keep the computer classes going, and much more. I think to myself, "Here is a man in the closing years of his life who is not looking to see gains for himself, but rather to see how he can be of help to others."

Before the day ends, I receive a call from a man in Ohio. He operates a chicken processing company and wants to donate 16 thousand pounds of frozen chicken to the poor in our area. However, it's going to require transporting it here, getting freezer space to store it, and, of course, arranging for vans and trucks to distribute it to the needy. Where will we find these resources? I wonder what challenge the next hour will bring.

A parishioner asked me today why and how I keep going with so much energy, when I am now working very hard on just being 77 years old.

I think about it too. I guess I only have one answer to the question, and that is God. He is the reason and the solution. I must fall in love with Him and then I must display that love. I call this love, "worship."

I must cry out morning and night that I love Him, that I will honor and serve Him, and that I will introduce Him to every person I meet. I will always put Him first. Worship is the most important and necessary duty of my day.

It is now 8:30 p.m. In the quiet of my back porch, our Lord speaks to me. "I am happy that your thoughts are at last turning to me not merely to ask and beg, but now to praise and extol. I am pleased with your priestly prayer, the breviary. It begins and ends each day of your life.

"The rosary that you carry not only reminds you of my faith and love, it also gets Jesus' mother at your side. She gave me more worship than any human being I have ever brought forth on this earth. I am sure with her help, you will worship better than you ever could by yourself.

"You also worship me in the physical work that you do. Remember how when Adam fell I said that he would earn his keep by the sweat of his brow? This was the way that he was to overcome sin, to make up to me for the hurt he had caused – through work.

"This week, I've seen you working very hard in the warehouses, organizing them, loading food onto trucks and distributing it. You have had to sweat a little and I'm happy to see that.

"You fixed and cleaned a donated car to give to one of the nuns who serves the poor in Martin County. You also worked very hard this week in terms of travel. You put in over 2,000 miles, not an easy task for a man your age.

"You also gave me worship by your preaching in church. You bring my word to the hearts and minds of people. You preach out of doors in hollows, on the radio, and on television. You're on audio tapes.

"The Mass that you say each day is certainly the highest form of worship that I could ask for.

"You help so many people of other faiths honor me in the buildings they have, through donations of organs, pews, religious books and other things they need. I am grateful for this worship that you give me through others.

"I admire the hard decision you made this week in Florida. After preaching for CAP in Fort Lauderdale, you had planned to visit some former volunteers in the Orlando area. Some of them had been volunteers as long as 40 years ago. You were looking forward so much to seeing them again! But when you learned of the death of your sister-in-law's mother, and that you were wanted for the funeral, you knew you had to go home.

"I am proud also of what you consider to be your most important work. Many say you are a fine preacher and the founder of a great organization. You are a good fundraiser and you've written many books. You've done much to be a humanitarian and to help others work together. But when you are asked what you think is your greatest contribution, you always say it is being a priest, a man who offers sacrifice to the most high.

"You tell the elderly that I have not forgotten them – that they have still the finest, most important time of their life left.

"You tell the poor that they must dream and not give up. They must do all in their power to pray and, with God's help, things will be better.

"You tell the rich that they are not important because of what they have, but because of what they are, and that they need to share and make the world a better place.

"You talk to the sick and tell them that their pain can be offered to God as one of the greatest contributions that they can make.

"To the young seeking to be successful, you challenge them that success is not the accumulation of wealth and power, but rather the accumulation of holiness, and the realization that they are ambassadors for Christ.

"I appreciate how you aren't afraid to speak up for me in public meetings. In the halls of state, county and federal governments, where my name is not to be mentioned, you are always there saying that without God, they can do nothing. And you always begin the prayer with the sign of the cross."

"But Lord," I interrupt, "these are nothing compared to what you give me each day: the Mass, that wonderful sacrifice that you made at the Last Supper and completed on the cross on Good Friday. You told your apostles, 'Do this in memory of me. Offer up this sacrifice to my father.' You have given me the privilege of being a part of that each day.

"I also think you are too generous in Your comments tonight," I add. "Don't You see the distractions in my prayer? Don't You see how sometimes when I am saying the rosary I get to the last step and I wonder, 'Where in the world has my mind been? How did I get to this last Mystery when I don't remember meditating on the others?'

"Volunteers and others come up to me often these days saying 'Father, let me help you. You might get hurt. Why don't you take it easy.' What they are really saying is, 'You are old. We'd better get in there and do the job so that it's done right.'"

By now it is 10:00 p.m. I get up from my chair and prepare for bed. I take out my book of Christian Heroes. Tonight I read about one of the earliest heroes, Saint Stephen.

His enemies cast heavy stones upon him, breaking his body. Still, he cried out that he hoped they would turn to Christ. Stephen gave his very life to worship God. As the stones beat him to the ground, he praised God and cried out, "Lord, do not hold this sin against them."

I have always thought in my own mind that Stephen was the one who converted Saint Paul. For Paul was that young man who watched over the coats of others as they threw the rocks that killed Stephen. And I am sure that once Stephen was in high heaven with God, he asked God time and again to bring this young man into the fold, to forgive him his impetuosity, and to give him the grace to know and love the Lord.

I close the book and put out the lights. "Stephen," I pray, "I so want to be like you. I want my life to express itself in worship as you did. Please remember me as you did Paul."

Stephen replies, "It is my experience that you are most likely to get what you pray for. Ask Jesus many times a day, 'Make me holy, Lord. Help me to worship your Father.'"

I turn over in bed. I am grateful this long and difficult week, this long and difficult day are done.

It has certainly not been easy. But isn't it great that God not only tells us what to do, he gives us saints to show and guide us?

Oh, Lord, I love you.

&

Chapter 8 The Love of Volunteers

If there was one thing that permeated my heart
and soul when I first came to Appalachia 50 years ago,
it was loneliness. There were more than 50,000 people
who lived in the neighboring counties, but I did not
know even one. I also never had the chance to meet
the nearest priest as he was in another county and was
busy ministering to his neighboring counties.

Every business place was strange to me and I had
no idea where to shop or where to go for assistance of
any kind.

To make matters worse, the old house that I
owned in Berea was in terrible shape. Also, looming
before me were the miles I would have to drive to seek
out and find the few Catholics in the area. The
prospect was staggering.

How could a young man – a 26 year old priest –
with so little experience possibly succeed? I'd always
been surrounded by family, by my church, and by a
multitude of friends. Now they were all taken away. I
was so alone. And it hurt.

If I was going to be productive, I had to dispel the
loneliness. I had to find companions.

My first step, of course, was to seek out Christ. Only He could give me real peace. He had to be my best friend and my closest companion. Thankfully, I did find Him, and He has been a great companion. He has never left my side.

Eventually, I found the few Catholics in my four counties but they were so scattered that they could not be a close source of strength for me. Plus, nearly half of them were children. And while I loved to play with children, there was little they could provide in the way of advice or strength.

To many in the local community, I represented a church whose teachings were very foreign. As a result, many people wanted nothing to do with me. What was I to do?

Volunteers, it seemed, were the only solution I had. I had to get people from outside of Appalachia to help me. They had to come at their own expense because I had so little to recompense them.

Before long, because of prayer and seeking out, a small group of volunteers began to come and stand at my side.

First it was my family. My mother and father were such powerful allies. They gathered up my 10 brothers and sisters, and their husbands and wives, and they made almost weekly trips down to help.

They also brought their friends along — Catholics and non-Catholics alike. People I had never known before were helping me nail the boards, paint the walls and fix the roof of my old house.

I went back to kids I had taught in high school and asked if they could come down during the summer and help me. They did come and they did help. We had so much fun! In the evenings, we drank soda, ate ice cream, sat around and told stories.

And how can I forget the members of the first parish I served in Dayton, KY right after ordination? They showed their love for me by coming and helping, bringing things and making life much more endurable.

Word began to spread. College students came from Lexington, then from Louisville and Cincinnati. They asked what they could do to help. Before long a procession was under way and I had to find places for them all to stay while they were here helping me.

Each of the counties I served had simple facilities, but we had to get these people some modicum of comfort. Sometimes it was simply a sleeping bag or mattress on the floor, or a bunk-bed thrown together. It was a "closely knit organization" in the sense that we lived so close together — and we shared so much!

The first volunteers would typically arrive on a Friday night and leave on Sunday afternoon. Then, as summer came, they would stay for a week at a time. It would be eight years before I got a volunteer who would stay longer than a month.

The first volunteer who stayed for a whole year came from Covington in Northern Kentucky. She had decided to come because a priest had said her service would be for a noble cause. At the time, I had no place for her to live. So I approached one of my parishioners who lived down the street behind the church, and she kindly agreed to let my volunteer live with her.

Most volunteers in those early days were young Catholics. All that would change as the years passed. We began attracting people who were older, and of other faiths.

One was a gentleman from Lexington named Bill Iille. He had worked the mountains, he had worked in timber, he had worked in lumber and various other occupations that had taken him from one side of Eastern Kentucky to the other. When he heard that I was trying to start a Catholic chapel in McKee in Jackson County, he knocked on my door one day, saying he wanted to see the Catholic priest.

I said I was he.

He said, "I have come to help you," to which I replied, "Why?" After all, we had never met before.

He replied, "I know this country. I have been here for years doing business. I know there are no Catholics here, and if anyone is coming here to try to start something new, they'd have to be crazy.

" My father always told me not to leave crazy people alone, but rather give them whatever help you can." Of course, his eyes smiled as he said these words and I knew his heart was genuine.

So it was that he began coming on Monday mornings and staying until Saturday afternoon, when he returned home to his wife. He helped me build so many things — camps, rummage stores, barns for cows and all the other things that we needed.

A special gift of gratitude is in my heart for Bellermine College in Louisville, Kentucky. Its students came, a few at a time – and then more – to offer their summers and their weekends as they had them. After a year or so, these special students took their message of what they had experienced in these mountains to the National Catholic College Association's annual convention. As a result of the students' positive report, more volunteers came – over a hundred for a week – and all needed accommodations.

I began to divide the volunteers up among the various counties where we had the most need. Although they were scattered, we always got together a night or two each week to recount the things we had done and the hopes that we had for the days that remained.

From the very beginning I established a deep personal relationship with the volunteers. Those that came for a week, or even for a weekend, usually arrived on a Friday evening. After they got settled as to where they were to sleep and work, where the bathrooms were, and where they would eat, we would gather together and I would speak to them.

I always started with a history of the area, sharing its beauty, promise and difficulties. I gave them a picture of what was going on here and now as well as some answers to the problems they would face. Then I shared with them my dreams of how we could bring blessings and hope to the people of Appalachia.

Next I outlined the tasks that they were to accomplish while they were here with CAP. I then asked each one to identify him- or herself – where each came from and his or her plans after college. I then opened the session to whatever questions they had.

Finally, after doing my best to answer their questions, I concluded with what I needed from them.

First, I needed their prayers and spiritual input. Without that, anything else they gave would be of little consequence. Without exception, their greatest reason for being there was to bring God with them and serve as His agent.

Their feeling was that God was the biggest worker, and that we had to be able to work beside and with Him.

Next, I needed their physical help in the communities. That required getting up at an early hour, working all day long, sweating, and coming home tired. I would remind them time and time again that "a happy volunteer was a tired volunteer."

Finally, I asked them when they returned to their homes to spread the news of what we were doing in the mountains. "Get other people interested," I beseeched them. "We need more volunteers. We need various things – things like tools, vehicles, lumber, clothes and so much more."

I reminded them they were to be ambassadors for Christ and for His poor. They were CAP's presence in the outside world, and I begged them not to forget the times they had spent with us.

Over the past 50 years, more than 50,000 volunteers have joined me in this work. It has been the largest

outpouring of volunteer help that any private organization has ever seen in this country.

I am often amazed at how many volunteers have
come to us, and how diverse and splendid they have
been – an enormous testimony to Christian vitality and
the American spirit. But they were more than that.

Our volunteers formed a bond of love so strong
and vital, it was impossible to express in mere words.

To this day, these caring, dedicated people seek to
solve problems wherever they are. They bring a religious maturity to everything they do. I see that in the
letters we receive. I see that in the people who come
to visit me who were volunteers in days gone by. I
think we have founded a community in a very real
sense; not a community that stays in a monastery, but
one that is spread out across the whole world.

Now, after 50 years, the number of volunteers is
growing. As we start the new millennium, we expect
1,500 "temporary" volunteers this year, who will come
from a week to four months. In addition, we will have
more than 100 "permanent" volunteers, who will commit at least a year of their time. Many of them stay
longer.

As I mentioned earlier, the first permanent volunteer was a young woman sent by a priest friend. I
arranged for her to live with a neighbor in Lancaster.

Then a college graduate, Mary Jo, came from
Cincinnati. She was a wonderful woman who stayed
for three years, and left only because I told her that
she had another vocation that she must answer.

Another group of volunteers that sticks out in my mind is a family from Cincinnati who initially came to our summer camp simply to visit my family with whom they were friends. A tragedy preceded their arrival. The father had died of a heart attack while working on New Year's Eve. During that first visit, the mother, Rita, and four of the five children, came down for the summer. Rita cooked for our camp, the older kids helped as counselors, and the littlest ones were campers.

Amazingly, Rita ended up staying on for 10 years, serving as a strong mother figure to so many volunteers, until a heart attack took her life as well.

As I look back on it now, I realize that CAP has had volunteers from every state in the Union, including Alaska and Hawaii. At least six or eight foreign countries have sent us volunteers as well.

Many retirees have volunteered with CAP, even some in their seventies. They want so much to be involved in a worthy cause.

In fact, I just attended the fiftieth wedding anniversary of one of the older couples who volunteer – George and Margaret. What a wonderful day that was! We had volunteers from Maine to Minnesota to Michigan to Florida helping them celebrate.

Many of our older volunteers not only share their skills, enthusiasm, and wealth of experience with CAP but also a part of their material wealth. They give us a portion of their stocks or bonds to develop programs in which they have particular interest.

Religious orders have also come to help, especially the Augustinians — folks like Liam, and Ed, and so many of their companions. In later years, some traveled as far as Japan, others to places in the U.S. like Arizona, taking what they had learned in the mountains and sharing it with people all over the earth.

There was a wonderful nun, Sister Sarah, who was also a nurse by profession. She, together with doctors who'd come in from Lexington, had the strength, enthusiasm and skills necessary to keep a local hospital from closing.

Then there was Marilyn, who stayed longer with CAP than any other volunteer. She came from a religious vocation in Connecticut, and remained 29 full years. She dedicated herself to so many things: setting up and running rummage stores, setting up child development centers; caring for the handicapped and much more.

I think of all the CAP volunteers who went on to religious vocations. Many of the young men now in seminary are studying not only to serve in dioceses, but also with missionary orders like Maryknoll. They will take the word of Christ all over the world. That is such an exciting thing!

The call to a religious life has come not only to Catholic volunteers but to non-Catholics. David, a wonderful young man who served with us in Inez, is now preparing for a Protestant ministry. Others from Protestant backgrounds have also told me that this will be their vocation.

From time to time, we have heard from volunteers who have gone into the service of their country. Louis Freeh, for example, was once a volunteer. Now he is the head of the FBI. I often get cards from him thanking me for the wonderment that came into his life when he volunteered for CAP in college.

Most volunteers have gone back to their homes and have contributed to the needs of their own areas. So I praise them, not just for the good they did in Appalachia, but also for the good they have given to their own communities.

Many of our volunteers stay on as CAP employees. Moe, for example, has been with us for more than 25 years. Many others have followed that same example. Once they come to Appalachia, they decide to stay and make a life for themselves, settling down, having children and raising families. These former volunteers instill in their own children the excitement of doing something special for Appalachia.

CAP volunteers have also been inspirations to the people already in our mountain communities. I see, for example, high school students now anxious to help other people. They originally came under a school program to help CAP build a camp. Now they want to reach beyond simply having jobs. They want to be volunteers.

There are teachers who, when they get done with their classes, come to CAP in the evenings and help teach those who haven't had an opportunity to learn.

A couple of state policeman came to CAP and said that they would help out in the evenings by forming a basketball team and providing other activities to help children stay on the straight and narrow.

I think these local volunteers have added a new dimension to the life of Appalachia. They have taken the focus away from the individual – what I want; what I need – and have redirected the focus to what can I give; what can I contribute?

"May I interrupt your story?" the Lord asks. "In my opinion, the greatest contribution that CAP has made to the betterment of Appalachia has been in its volunteers. Their strength and importance have not just been in their abilities, their hard work or their contribution of material things. What I see coming out of them more than anything has been their love. They have had a great love for me and for my people.

"As well as you know the volunteers, you have no idea of the depth of their love. It's not easy for many of them to be at church at 7:15 a.m. Do you realize how many of them take a holy hour in the church each day? Do you how many of them spend time in prayer during the day in their own private rooms and in the quiet of their own lives?

"Many of them make great sacrifices. They separate themselves from their families and children, and they oftentimes are lonely. But it is their love that makes all the difference. Their love makes the difference.

"I don't know if you notice," the Lord says, "how many of your volunteers are older people, and how many come from religious groups other than your own.

"I am pleased to see the people of so many generations and so many faiths. This is a wonderful way in which you get to know and respect each other. It is an important step in bringing all of My people together in unity again."

"Lord," I say, "I had no idea when I was so lonely and prayed to You for companions that You would respond with such magnificence. The gift of volunteers is the most outstanding gift of love I have ever seen."

"That's the reason I am God," the Lord says. "I have all the answers to your problems and to the world's problems. I have the power to bring about everything that is good.

"By the way," the Lord says, "I am thankful that you have learned to volunteer yourself. I know you could have retired at 65. You are now 76. And I know the other day you volunteered to the bishop to continue as an active priest until you are at least 80. You're on the right track. Just keep it up."

"But Lord" I say, "I have problems. You see, I still want to do my own thing. I want to chart my own course. I need to be more humble, for humility is the true source of love. Help me, Lord to serve and not to be served and waited on."

"Have I not always answered your prayers? I am always ready," says the Lord. "I give you this advice. Remember the last day of Jesus' life when he had to turn to me and say, 'Your will be done. Your will to come and not my own'? Make that your daily prayer.

"By the way," the Lord says, "have you seen the clock? It is nearly midnight. I wish you would go to sleep. I need a good day's volunteer work out of you tomorrow."

As I go to bed, I once again open my book of Christian Heroes. My subject tonight is Maximillian Kolby, a Franciscan priest. He had gone to Japan, where he had helped to build a congregation in Nagasaki. (Many of the congregation were later killed by the atomic bomb.) He returned to Poland when Hitler took control, and he was imprisoned in the concentration camp at Dachau.

The Nazis warned that each time a person attempted to escape, 10 people would be killed. One man who had been so selected for execution cried out that he had a wife and children. Maximillian Kolby heard his cries. He stepped forward, saying he would die in his stead. And he did.

I close the book. What a great figure of a volunteer you were, Maximillian! You volunteered your own life to save that of another. Please help me to be as generous as you were.

"Just do the little things each day," he replies. "When a larger task is asked of you, you will be ready."

I say a prayer for those 50,000 and more volunteers who have taken away my loneliness. "Lord, fill them with love. Let their cup runneth over. I love them all so very much."

Chapter 9 The Love of the Land

When I think of love and Appalachia, I always
wind up with the love of the land. I have never seen
people so in love with the land in which they were
born and raised. They've demonstrated this great love
on many occasions.

I remember I was preaching in Breathitt County.
The Army Corps of Engineers had re-routed the
Kentucky River and created a wonderful place where
business was going to thrive someday. I wanted so
much to obtain a beautiful piece of land there to build
the county's first Catholic church.

I found out who owned the land and asked the
man if he would show it to me. He told me right off
that many had tried to buy the parcel, but it was not
for sale. I asked that he show it to me anyway, and he
did. After the tour of his property, he said to me,
"What do you think?"

I replied, "I think it is the most beautiful sight I
have seen in the county. It's a lovely place. You have a
wonderful piece of land here."

He looked at me in surprise and said, "You're not
too smart in buying land, are you? Everybody else who

wants it points out all the shortcomings, yet you come along and say you think it's beautiful. You know, there's only one thing the Lord ain't making more of, and that's land.

"I'll tell you what," he said. "Because you love the land, because you said a good thing about it, I'll sell you this property."

Today, a Catholic Church stands on that land because this man loved the land and I did too. It's because of that mutual love that we became friends.

On a different occasion, I was in Breathitt County to do some street preaching. I had asked the community if I could preach on a bridge that crossed the north fork of the Kentucky River.

They said, "Oh, that wouldn't be a good idea."

To which I responded, "Why?"

They explained that there had been a duel on that bridge. Two men had come at each other with guns, drawn and fired. Each hit their mark and each was killed.

They had been fighting over land. Supposedly one man put his fence one foot over onto the other man's property, saying it was his. Because they had such strong feelings for the land, they defended it to the death.

I remember another time in Harlan County during one of the most severe floods in nearly 30 years. I was bringing food and clothing, and helping clean up the rubble. I went to the water-damaged home of a frail old woman and offered her some food. She hesitated, but the more we talked, the more friendly we became. After some time I asked her, "What will your future be, now that your home has been devastated?"

She said, "My children want to me move away to Middlesborough or even to Lexington."

"Will you go?" I asked

"Oh no. I'm not going."

"Why not?"

"Look up there on the hill," she said. "My man is buried there. This is his land and mine, and I'm not gonna leave him. I'm gonna stay."

In recent years, I've seen rather nice houses built in the hills. They are being built by people who moved away and were gone for 20, 30 or more years. They saved enough money for retirement and decided that they wanted to spend the last years of their lives in the peace of the land from which they came.

There is an affection — a bond — between people and the soil. Sometimes it is hard to understand. Our mountains in Eastern Kentucky are not the tallest in Appalachia. They only get as tall as 4,000 feet, and that in only one spot in Harlan County. Mostly they are no more than 2,000 feet high. But the hills have a habit of being almost one on top of the other, separated by creeks and rivers flowing through tiny valleys.

You feel surrounded, but in a good, not a threatening, way. The hills seem there to protect you and give you comfort. They are your guardians and your strength.

You somehow feel that the streams and the hills are a part of you just as you are a part of them.

This has been so from the beginning. My great hero of Appalachia is Daniel Boone. He was one of the very first white men to explore these mountains. One of his great desires was to have some of this land to share with his children and grandchildren. He had such a fondness for this land.

And yet, he would know such disappointment. Of the nearly 9,000 acres of land granted to him for his great exploits in Kentucky, not one single acre was his when he left in 1799.

He was more disappointed over that than anything else in his life.

Similarly, Kentucky's other pioneers would endure almost everything if they could only have the land, if it could only be a part of their heritage.

Yet, the land and its future are very much in doubt today.

We here in Appalachia are about at the end of the coal phase of our history. The coal is running out and the workforce is declining. During 100 years of coal mining, much damage has been done to the land. There is erosion, and the piles of silts are monstrous to see. Great gouges have been cut into the hills, and hollows have been flooded. All in all, the land has not fared well.

We wonder what industry will come into these mountains to sustain our people and give them a livelihood that is filled with dignity.

If our area were to pursue some of the more conventional means of industrialization, it would mean erecting major roadways. But these would be so expensive as the mountains are so hard to level. Even our current roads are hard to care for.

Will the land be able to support its people? A new challenge upon us as this new millennium breaks is pollution — not merely from the coal mines and their activities, but from our people themselves.

Let me explain.

The early towns were built by the coal mining companies. They owned the houses, the streets and all the facilities. There were no local partners. The local people were not trained nor made to be a part of that component of their life. The mine managers made sure everything was running properly. Frequently, they did a very good job.

There is now, however, a vacuum of trained leadership to keep our towns looking beautiful and protect the land.

Compounding the problem, in recent years we have entered into a fast-food, throw-away society.

What do you do with the bags and packages that your lunch comes in? What do you do with old, broken-down cars? What do you do with the cans that soft drinks and beer come in? What do you do with refrigerators that don't keep things cold any longer, or stoves that no longer heat? What do you do with furniture that is no longer usable?

For so long a time, we have had no county-wide garbage service. Instead, people have become accustomed to dumping their trash wherever they could.

"Throw it into the creek, it will wash away" they reason.

We have cluttered our land with trash and filth. We have despoiled our beautiful mountains and streams for so long that it has become a rule of life.

But in recent years, there have been some wonderful signs of improvement. The Army Corps of Engineers has done a marvelous task of creating beautiful lakes throughout our mountains. Not only do these lakes protect our towns from being flooded and from our land being washed away, but they have encouraged recreation like camping and boating. I think this has been one of the greatest contributions we have had.

These lakes stretch from one part of Appalachia to the other. They're small in comparison to those in Western Kentucky, but they are filled with the majesty of mountains and the beauty of sunrise and the grandeur of sunset. There is no nicer place to be when evening comes than in a boat on that water.

The forestry departments — both the state and federal — have tried to preserve the forest. They insist that campers can't indiscriminately start fires. They insist that timbering be done with reason and moderation, and that there be sensible replanting of trees to make the hills fruitful again.

Our State of Kentucky is taking seriously the preservation and restoration of beauty. The Governor,

Paul E. Patton, an Eastern Kentuckian himself, has made it one of his great priorities. He has appointed a wonderful man as Secretary of the Environment and Natural Resources, General Brickford. Originally from Harlan County, he is dedicated to making people aware of their responsibilities to keep the land free of trash.

This state effort is joined by a federal effort as well. We have a wonderful man in Congress by the name of Hal Rogers. In recent years he has begun a program called 'Operation Pride.' Its purpose is to make people aware that the mountains should be a place of beauty and not a place to dump, litter, and spoil. He has worked hard going across county, political and other lines to say to us all, "Let us join together and renew the face of God's earth." Beautiful things are happening as a result.

We at CAP have been trying for years to do our part. In the Bible schools, one of the things that we teach is that if the children love God, they have to love God's land. From the very beginning God gave mankind the duty of overseeing the earth and seeing to it that it would carry out its appointed destiny, which was to be a thing of beauty.

We try to instill the same idea into the children that come to our camps. Almost every one of our camps is on a lake. Without fail, we take the kids out on a boat during their stay and one of their tasks is to pick up the trash along the banks in plastic bags.

Then we have our young people in teen centers. Besides helping them with their studies and giving them wholesome recreation, we encourage them to clean up their neighborhoods and to get together with other people to see what they can do to make it more beautiful.

We don't neglect this topic either in the GED classes, where people who are older work on getting their high school equivalency diploma. We say to them that as part of their renewed spirit of learning, they must be leaders — that they must be the ones who really and truly show others how our land can be preserved and beautified.

We have to make the beautiful happen, and then the ugly will disappear. If people are part of beautification, they won't pollute and destroy.

"Oh Lord," I say, "you need to put more effort into beautification. Send more grace to the people, that they will see the advantages of what their land would have if they only cared for it.

" Can't you make companies understand that they have a responsibility to the land from which they make their profit? Can't you make people realize that throwing out trash and collecting junk is not a virtue? That it belittles them as well as the land?"

Somehow I always get into this kind of mood at the end of the day. The images have built up through my travels, and the sadness sets in.

"You always want things to happen overnight, don't you?" the Lord replies. "The ravages and neglect of 100 years, you want corrected overnight. It just isn't going to happen that way. I'm not going to do the work myself. I'm not going to work a miracle. All you need to do is chip in and do your part.

"Don't you think I haven't entered into the hearts and minds of the people you just described in your manuscript, people who have made so much effort to make this land into a thing of beauty again? Don't you think I have been behind the making of the lakes, and the forest improvements, and the state and federal efforts? The people who have espoused these causes were all moved by me.

"Be patient. My people are changing. They are getting a clear picture of what this land can be like.

"You just keep on trying. Keep working. The time and day of success are mine to determine, not yours."

I know his words apply to so many other questions of mine as well. Once again I know He is right. God is so wise and powerful and full of love. What would we ever do without Him?

"Lord," I say, "be patient also, and push us and push me. Don't let us be ordinary. Keep pushing us to make good come about."

I say the final prayers of the night and go to bed. My book of heroes is on the night stand.

My friend for the night is Moses. He is a hero to those of the Christian faith.

He led the Israelites out of Egypt, the land of slavery. He took them through the Red Sea, out into the desert. He saw the bareness of the desert and yet he saw the beauty of the mountains as well. He led his

Jewish people to the Promised Land flowing with milk and honey. He brought them home.

He saw this Promised Land only from a distance. Another man, Joshua, would lead them into it. But without Moses, they wouldn't have been at the gates of Jericho seeking entrance.

Moses had brought them there with their love of the land. With the promise of the Promised Land, they could endure 40 years of hardship.

"Moses," I say, "give me your faith, your patience, and your endurance, that someday I can help the people of Appalachia build a land of milk and honey, a land where beauty finds itself so much at home."

"Plant a flower every day," Moses tells me. "Pick up a piece of trash. Speak to everyone of beauty. The Lord will help you as He did me. You may not see that day come round, but someday it will come round if you don't lose heart."

I turn out the light and the day is closed. "Lord," I say, "I hope I live a long time yet. I so want to help. But Your schedule is the best, so just let me do the best I can. And please, when the curtain is finally drawn, bring me to that land of Yours where beauty and love endure forever.

"Until we meet again, dear Lord, thank you. Thank you very much."

Epilogue

Two years ago, I met with some of the leaders of CAP and told them that I thought the next three books should prepare us for the millennium that was to come.

I thought that Faith, Hope and Love should be the themes of the books. And so we followed that course.

This book completes that effort. We are now in the new millennium. Its course is hidden from our eyes, but I am convinced that these three great virtues will enable us to make it a time of special meaning and great promise.

This book is the twelfth one I have written in as many years. So many of you have written and said how you enjoy them, and how they have made a change in your life. I am so grateful for such letters. I am humbled to see how much good they have been able to do for you.

So many of our CAP volunteers tell us that the books were their entrance into CAP, and that they became volunteers because of the spirit that they found in the books. I am so pleased about that as well.

Just this week, I received a letter from a bank in Covington, KY. They were responsible for a trust fund set up by a woman who had just passed away. She had been reading the books for years and fell in love with what we were doing. She wanted that love to be real, and so she left us a considerable amount of money in the trust.

This has happened to us time and time again. The books have profited and assisted the people in Appalachia a very great deal.

When I write these books, I don't ever imagine I am writing to a crowd, or to faceless people in general. I intend them to be more like letters that I will send to someone I love.

I so want you to see the challenges of Appalachia. I also have hope that you will help me to overcome them. I so want to make a difference. Your prayers, the sacrifices you offer, and the financial support you send have literally changed our mountains and our people.

In the last two books, I deliberately tried to become more united with you. I spoke more plainly about the great love of my life, which is Christ. I shared with you my dreams and my sadness.

I let you into my heart, where God and I do battle and are reconciled each day. I wanted you to know how deeply I appreciate the heroes who have gone before me and have so affected my desire to love God more and more.

I didn't want this story to get too sentimental, but I did want you to know how human and frail I am.

I don't have all the answers. I stumble and fall like all my brothers and sisters. I need your help and support. I open my heart with the hope that you will enter therein.

When I was about 22 years old, I put in a special prayer to the Lord. "Could I please live to see the 21st century?" I asked. My birthday was January 1, 1924, so I asked to be 76. January of this year I was 76, and I have seen the new century.

I wonder how the prayer will continue to be answered and what its end will be. Is this the last year of my life, or has God got more time for me? I suspect he has, since I have so much for which I have to make up! It would take a lot of time to make up for all of the sins and imperfections for which I've been responsible.

Whatever is to be, I am satisfied that God has been so good and has brought me so many wonderful friends. So, for the time being, I say farewell to you all.

It has been a good life, and 50 years in the mountains has been a grace I didn't dare hope for. I hope you will remember me, for surely I will never forget you.

Books on Tape

Many of you have asked me to record the books on tape.

During this past year, I have recorded all of the books. They are in attractive plastic cases and have two 90-minute tapes each. Each set represents one book. If you would like to obtain one or more of the books, please write or call the CAP office.

Christian Appalachian Project
322 Crab Orchard Street
Lancaster, KY 40446
606-792-3051

The Mountain Spirit

Our bimonthly magazine The Mountain Spirit, will keep you up-to-date on the work of the Christian Appalachian Project as we continue to help the people of this poverty-stricken area help themselves. In the magazine, you will also find moving, inspiring stories about the people we serve. If you would like to subscribe to this publication, please complete the order form below.

THE MOUNTAIN SPIRIT — Subscription Order Form

Please send me CAP's magazine *The Mountain Spirit*. Subscription rate: One year - $8.00.

Name_____

Address_____

City_____State_____Zip_____

E-mail Address_____

One of Father Beiting's dreams is to personally share his vision with you and your church or civic group. For more information on available dates for him to speak with your group, please contact: W. Ben Prewitt, Special Assistant to Father Beiting, at Christian Appalachian Project, 322 Crab Orchard Street, Lancaster, KY 40446-0001, or call (606) 792-3051. ext. 284. www.chrisapp.org.

Dear Father Beiting,

____ I am interested in helping to fulfill your dreams
for Appalachia. Please contact me.

____ Please contact me to arrange for a visit from a
CAP representative.

____ Please send me free literature about opportunities
for making planned gifts to CAP.

____ Please send me information about CAP's
Endowment Fund.

Name_____

Address_____

City_____State_____Zip_____

E-mail Address_____

Mail this form to: W. Ben Prewitt, Special Assistant to
Father Beiting, at Christian Appalachian Project, 322
Crab Orchard Street, Lancaster, KY 40446-0001

I am interested in volunteering with the Christian Appalachian Project

Please send me information about:

☐ One-year volunteer opportunities
(year round admissions)

☐ Summer Camp volunteer opportunities
(June - August)

☐ Short-term volunteer opportunities
(September - May)

Name_____

Address_____

City_____State_____Zip_____

E-mail Address_____

Please return this form to and/or contact us at:

> Christian Appalachian Project
> Volunteer Recruitment
> 322 Crab Orchard Street
> Lancaster, KY 40446-0001
> E-mail: volunteer@chrisapp.org.

A summary of the registration and financial documents filed by this organization can be obtained by contacting: in Maryland, for the cost of copies and postage, the Secretary of State, State House, Annapolis, MD 21401; in Virginia, State Division of Consumer Affairs, P.O. Box 1163, Richmond, VA 23209; in Washington, residents can call the Secretary of State toll-free within the state, 800-332-4483; in Mississippi, by calling the Secretary of State's office at 888-236-6167; IN NEW YORK, OFFICE OF THE ATTORNEY GENERAL, CHARI-TIES BUREAU, 120 BROADWAY, NEW YORK, NY 10271; IN NEW JERSEY, THE ATTORNEY GENERAL BY CALLING 973-504-6215; IN PENNSYLVANIA, DEPARTMENT OF STATE BY CALLING TOLL-FREE WITHIN THE STATE, 800-732-0999; IN WEST VIR-GINIA, SECRETARY OF STATE, STATE CAPITOL, CHARLESTON, WV 25305; IN FLORIDA, THE DIVISION OF CONSUMER SERVICES BY CALLING TOLL-FREE WITHIN THE STATE, 800-435-7352; IN NORTH CAROLINA, FINANCIAL INFORMATION AND A COPY OF THE LICENSE ARE AVAIL-ABLE FROM THE STATE SOLICITATION LICENSING BRANCH AT 1-888-830-4989, OR OUTSIDE THE STATE AT 919-807-2214; or by writing the Christian Appalachian Project, 322 Crab Orchard Street, Lancaster, KY 40446-0001. Our license number in Michigan is MICS9933. Registration with any of the above government agencies does not imply endorsement by the state.

To learn more about the Christian Appalachian Project, visit our website at www.chrisapp.org